ENTERTAINING YOUR ANGELS

The Secret to Understanding God's Angelic Hosts

Master Prophet E. Bernard Jordan

FOGHORN
PUBLISHERS
"Of Making Many Books There Is No End..."

Entertaining Your Angels: The Secret to Understanding God's Angelic Hosts

ISBN-10: 1-934466-28-X
ISBN-13: 978-1-934466-28-5

Printed in the United States of America
©2010 by E. Bernard Jordan. All Rights Reserved.

Foghorn Publishers
P.O. Box 8286
Manchester, CT 06040-0286
860-216-5622
www.foghornpublisher.com
foghornpublisher@aol.com

Juergen Bruschkewitz

Table of Contents

Prophetic Partner

For the past two decades I have been totally committed to helping transform our world for the better through *The Power of Prophecy* and also through my written publications. We have found that the principle of the seed is the most effective way to saturate the universe with a much-needed word. To that end, I have freely given away thousands of books free of charge. This altruistic effort has been made possible through the generous support from caring people such as yourself, my prophetic partner.

There are so many wonderful treasures that God has given me, and I want to give them back to you. Will you help me? Will you stand with the Master Prophet by supporting the furtherance of this prophetic message to the ends of the earth? I want your name to be listed in the next printing of this book. I believe that you will help me to help thousands of other hungry souls by sowing your prophetic seed into my publishing ministry. The blessing that will come to you as a result of your seed sown will continue to speak for generations to come.

Yes Master Prophet, I

Am committed to helping you fulfilling God's purpose in your life through publishing books that bring life to all that read them! You can count on me.

Introduction

Angels are Men

"Then there came again and touched me one like the appearance of a man, and he strengthened me, And said, O man greatly beloved, fear not: peace be unto thee, be strong, yea, be strong. And when he had spoken unto me, I was strengthened, and said, Let my lord speak; for thou hast strengthened me." (Daniel 10:18-19)

They Look Just Like You!

Angels are divine messengers from God sent to us to help bring forth prosperity, peace, power, greatness, wealth, good health and joy. If we are in tune with our angels, they speak to us on a daily basis to help unfold and reveal the plan and the purpose of God for our lives. Contrary to popular belief, angels do not appear as little, fat babies or beings with wings. The artistic portrayal of angels as winged beings lacks Biblical basis, except when reference is made to the seraphim and cherubim. Angels are mysterious messengers of God. In the earth realm, angels appear as men. They look, sound and move like you and me. However, if you are not in tune with the mind of God, you may not recognize the angels that are hovering right in your midst.

Angels are also thoughts embodied in man. Angels are sent directly from God and appear in human form. They come to illuminate your dreams, hopes and desires and to help validate and fulfill the word of the Lord for your life. Oftentimes in scripture, the angel of the Lord is described as the Lord Himself. However, there are many others readily available to aid human kind. Prophecy angels, prosperity angels, protection angels, healing angels, faith angels and so many more are just "waiting in the wings," so to speak, waiting for you to call them into your experience and put them on assignment.

Principle #1

Angels appear in your life to illuminate your
dreams, hopes and desires and to help validate
and fulfill the word of the Lord for your life.

Your blessings on earth will always come through a human being, people whom God has sent and ordained just for you. They are your angels. The angels whom God assigns to you have a significant role to play in your life. They will not appear with wings and halos. They will appear as Spirit manifested within the body of man. If angels appeared in our lives in any other form, we may be afraid of them and we may even reject their guidance and direction. However, when they manifest in our presence with an identity similar to ours—two arms, two legs, two eyes, a mouth, a nose—we are more apt to receive their information, guidance and direction.

> *"I lifted up mine eyes again, and looked, and behold a man with a measuring line in his hand. Then said I, Whither goest thou? And he said unto me, To measure Jerusalem, to see what is the breadth thereof, and what is the length thereof. And, behold, the angel that talked with me went forth, and another angel went out to meet him." (Zechariah 2:1-3)*

Angels will usually inspire awe, but sometimes they can be very unassuming. Oftentimes, in scripture, the appearance of the angels of the Lord in the lives of people is prefaced by saying, "Fear not." An angel can appear as a stranger, one who you would not expect to be the keeper of your blessing. Hebrews 13:2 says, *"Be not forgetful to entertain strangers, for many have entertained angels unawares."* Do not be forgetful to entertain strangers. Why? Because thereby, by taking the time to entertain strangers, some people have unknowingly entertained angels. Some people have had long and profound conversations with strangers while being completely unaware that they were really interacting with angels from God in disguise. As far as they knew, they had just been talking to a strange man or a strange woman, but in reality, they had just been interacting with an angel. So, how can we distinguish between a normal interaction with an average person and a direct contact with an angelic being? There is a litmus test that you can perform to help you identify those strangers that are really divine messengers sent by God. Whenever God sends angels into your life, they usually come to multiply some aspect of your life. Ask yourself the question, "What has multiplied in my life?" When you identify multiplication in your life, you have identified a moment in which you were touched by an angel.

Principle #2

Angels come into your life to multiply you.

Have you ever had money just appear in your hands, unexpected money, or had a check just appear in your mailbox or in your bank account? You were touched by an angel. Have you ever started out with something small and then, all of a sudden, it started to increase and multiply? You were touched by an angel. Have you ever seen a door that was closed in your life suddenly open, and seen that which you were praying for suddenly manifest itself in your experience? You were touched by an angel.

There are angels who are specifically assigned to you. They are sent by God to perform miracles on your behalf. They may appear as strangers, but they are divine messengers sent by God, who are busy carrying out God's assignment for your life. There are angels at your door. However, you must ask God to give you the presence of mind to recognize their appearance in your life.

The Angel of Increase

> *"And the angel of the LORD said unto her, I will multiply thy seed exceedingly, that it shall not be numbered for multitude. And the angel of the LORD said unto her, Behold, thou art with child and shalt bear a son, and shalt call his name Ishmael; because the LORD hath heard thy affliction. And he will be a wild man; his hand will be against every man, and every man's hand against him; and he shall dwell in the presence of all his brethren. (Genesis 16:10-12)*

Angels are sent to multiply the good in your life and to alleviate that which concerns you. Angels' appearance signal that multiplication is happening all around you. Therefore, do not provoke your angels. God sends His angels in your life to bless you.

> *"Behold, I send an Angel before thee, to keep thee in the way, and to bring thee into the place which I have prepared. Beware of him, and obey his voice, provoke him not; for he will not pardon your transgressions: for my name is in him." (Exodus 23:20-21)*

Exodus 23:20-21, makes it clear that you should not provoke your angels. Your angels are standing by watching to make sure that you enter into the divine increase that God ordained for your life. Unlike others you may meet along this journey called life, your angels have your best interest in mind. There is a fight for your life happening in the Spirit realm. The enemy is on assignment to deter you from your destiny, and he is not giving up. The enemy knows that God has "angels waiting in the outfield" to deliver you from the hands of destruction, fear, doubt, insecurity, depression and low self-esteem. But God sends His angels into your life so that you can see God and truly live. The enemy does not play fair, but he is no match for our God.

Principle #3

Do not provoke your angels.

God sends His angels to your life to usher you into the place that has been prepared for you. God wants to open the windows of heaven for you so that you can live a blessed, prosperous, healthy, happy and fulfilled life. Therefore, He sends His angels of increase so you may experience His divine favor, blessings, miracles, signs, wonders and prosperity.

> *"For he shall give his angels charge over thee, to keep thee in all thy ways. They shall bear thee up in their hands, lest thou dash thy foot against a stone."* (Psalms 91:11-12)

Angels only appear to the righteous. Angels were never known to appear to wicked people, only to those viewed within the Bible as good (for example, Abraham, Moses, David, Daniel, Jesus, Peter and Paul). They are charged with caring for God's people and serving them in times of need. If an angel appears in your life, know that you are numbered among the righteous. The angels witness to those who are heirs of salvation. Your angels will bear you up. They are always at work on your behalf.

Psalms 148:1-5 says, *"Praise ye the LORD. Praise ye the LORD from the heavens: praise him in the heights. Praise ye him, all his angels: praise ye him, all his hosts. Praise ye him, sun and moon: praise him, all ye stars of light. Praise him, ye heavens of heavens, and ye waters that be above the heavens. Let them praise the name of the LORD: for he commanded, and they were created."* God commanded and the angels were created. When God speaks a thing it is so. You don't have to worry about it. You don't have to second-guess it. It is so! It shall happen! Your angel will appear in your life to let you know that you have found favor with God. Favor signifies multiplication.

Principle #4

Favor signifies multiplication.

"And the angel came in unto her, and said, Hail, thou that art highly favoured, the Lord is with thee: blessed art thou among women. And when she saw him, she was troubled at his saying, and cast in her mind what manner of salutation this should be. And the angel said unto her, Fear not, Mary: for thou hast found favour with God." (Luke 1:28-3030)

It is one thing to find favor with God. But to be highly favored is an entirely different thing. There are different levels of favor. "Highly favored" means the Most High is favoring your condition. When you are highly favored, you are "with child." In a sense, you have been impregnated by the Spirit. Something has been implanted inside of you that is preparing to bring you into a season of longevity. Favor may result in an uncommon door that opens for you. But "highly favored" indicates that God himself steps in and says, "I want in on this one."

Mary had to make a distinction between these levels of favor. She said she was "blessed and highly favored." She was really saying, "The hand of God is upon me." It is not a "Man" thing. It is a God thing. Say with me, "I am ready for High Favor," favor from the Most High. In other words, favor cannot emanate from any higher place than that.

> *"And the angel of the LORD found her by a fountain of water in the wilderness, by the fountain in the way to Shur. And he said, Hagar, Sarai's maid, whence camest thou? and whither wilt thou go? And she said, I flee from the face of my mistress Sarai. And the angel of the LORD said unto her, Return to thy mistress, and submit thyself under her hands. And the angel of the LORD said unto her, I will multiply thy seed exceedingly, that it shall not be numbered for multitude. And the angel of the LORD said unto her, Behold, thou art with child and shalt bear a son, and shalt call his name Ishmael; because the LORD hath heard thy affliction." (Genesis 16:7-11)*

Your angels are dispatched in your life to multiply your seed. God has given angels the ability to bring forth multiplication in all aspects of your life. If you acknowledge your angels, then they can do that which they were assigned to do, which is to bring forth multiplication and increase in your life. The key is acknowledging, recognizing their presence and actions. The Bible says we are to acknowledge God in all our ways and he will direct our path. (Proverbs 3:6)

Principle #5

Your angels are dispatched in your life to multiply your seed.

Your angels are waiting in the wings to be invoked in your life. But, in order to call upon them, you have to be aware that your angels even exist. Sometimes we provoke our angels. This provocation can hinder their ability to prepare us to dwell in, and enjoy, the place God has ordained for our lives. Your angel will not pardon your transgressions. Therefore, whenever there is a word that is not fulfilling itself in your life, don't look at the prophet and say, "The prophet missed it." Examine your life and say, "Where am I missing it? What part am I missing that is keeping me from the promise? Where have I provoked my angels?"

Your angels have charge over you. Psalms 91:11-12 says, *"For he shall give his angels charge over thee, to keep thee in all thy ways. They shall bear thee up in their hands, lest thou dash thy foot against a stone."* When you understand that your angels have charge over you, you will begin to recognize that your angels are ready to work for you, in you and through you.

1

The Anatomy of Angels

The Spiritual Hierarchy

Angels are Spirit beings. They have their own rules of engagement and operate according to God's divine plan. Because of their mysterious and complex nature, people often misunderstand their purpose and importance in their lives. There is a spiritual hierarchy for celestial beings that has been established in scripture, and that is followed throughout the Old and New Testaments. This hierarchy can be divided into three tiers. The first tier serves as heavenly counselors—Cherubim, Seraphim and Thrones; the second tier serves as heavenly governors—Dominions, Virtues and Powers; and the third tier serves as heavenly messengers—Principalities, Angels and Archangels.

The **Seraphim**, the highest-ranked of the order in heaven, surround the throne of God, worshipping and declaring the glory of God, crying, "Holy, Holy, Holy is the Lord of hosts." (Isaiah 6:2-3).

The **Cherubim** are known as the guardians of light and the stars. The prophet Ezekiel saw four cherubim, described as having four faces and four wings. The cherubim cover the throne or the glory of God. (Ezekiel 1:10-11)

The **Thrones** are the judiciary angels who administer divine judgment. They ensure that God's truth is imparted in the lives of those who need it. (Colossians 1:16)

The **Dominions** integrate the spiritual and the material worlds. They determine cosmic responsibility. (Colossians 1:16)

The **Virtues** are known to emanate divine energy into the universe. It is their duty to bring forth the revelation of the miracles, signs and wonders of God.

The **Powers** bear the conscience of all humanity and help to cast out people's evil thoughts and deeds.

The **Principalities** are guardian angels to large groups of people. Entire nations and races are entrusted to them.

Principle #6

Angels have their own rules of engagement
and operate according to God's divine plan.

The **Archangels** are the voices of good news. (Michael, Gabriel, Raphael and Uriel). They deliver messages of hope, increase, and power.

The Angels are closest to humanity and are most concerned with the affairs of humans. Angels are humble because they do what they are told and cannot attribute the glory unto themselves. Yet, angels have enormous responsibility for interacting between God and mankind. Guardian angels are included in this category.

Praying to Your Angels

Some people may consider it idolatrous to pray to angels rather than directly to God. But Pope Pius XI (1857–1939) prayed to his guardian angel twice a day. Whenever he had to speak to someone who he thought may not accept his ideas, he first invoked his guardian angel to speak to the other person's guardian angel. The goal was to have the two guardian angels come to an understanding prior to the meeting. This allowed everything to proceed without difficulty. Since angels are assigned to bring the best to humankind, Pope Pius XI left the negotiations up to their guardian angels. He knew they would establish an interaction and communication that would work out for the good of all involved.

St. Ambrose (339–397), a fourth century Church father, believed that people should pray to their guardian angels. According to St. Ambrose, praying to angels does not constitute an act of worship towards them. It is simply a request for the angels to intercede on your behalf.

Principle #7

Angels are assigned to bring the best to humankind.

Praying to an angel is synonymous to asking someone to do you a favor. You are not revering them. You are simply making a request for their assistance. The simple act of talking to someone does not immediately imply that worship is taking place. Therefore, when you talk to your angels, you are not worshipping them. You are simply communicating your requests and invoking their assistance on your behalf. In fact, what you are really doing is praying with your angel, who will then deliver your prayer to the Most High God.

Angels are a part of the universal mind. Therefore, when you pray to your angels, you are praying to God. Including specific angels in your prayers is very powerful and effective. You might ask your guardian angels to deliver your prayers for you. You might also invoke the assistance of a specific angel who has a deep involvement with the topic of your prayer.

The Archangel Raphael is considered a healing angel. The Angel Muriel is one of the guardian angels and can be invoked whenever your emotions are out of alignment and need to be brought under control. The Angel Gazardiel is responsible for the sunrise. This angel is invoked for a new start or a new beginning. The Archangel Michael is invoked when strength and courage are needed or when you need to call on the liberating angel to free you from the hand of a situation that has you bound.

> *"For he shall give his angels charge over thee, to keep thee in all thy ways. They shall bear thee up in their hands, lest thou dash thy foot against a stone. Thou shalt tread upon the lion and adder: the young lion and the dragon shalt thou trample under feet. Because he hath set his love upon me, therefore will I deliver him: I will set him on high, because he hath known my name. He shall call upon me, and I will answer him: I will be with him in trouble; I will deliver him, and honour him. With long life will I satisfy him, and shew him my salvation."* (Psalm 91:11-16)

Your angels are always working with you. When a situation or circumstance arises in your life that needs clarification, you might receive help in the form of a dream. Sometimes your angels will send you a series of apparent coincidences which will ensure the right outcome. These apparent coincidences are really subtle messages to you from your angels. For example, someone may say to you, "I don't know why I am sharing this with you, but I was in a business deal with Mr. X and he did not pay me back my money." You may be getting ready to go into business with Mr. X, or an offer is getting ready to be made to you, so your angel orchestrates this meeting and conversation to keep you safe in all your ways. Your angels are always speaking to you and orchestrating the way information is filtered to you.

Principle #8

Apparent coincidences are really subtle messages to you from your angels.

Ministering Spirits

> *"Are they not all ministering spirits, sent forth to minister*
> *for them who shall be heirs of salvation?" (Hebrews 1:14)*

Angels are always at work. They are ministering spirits. They aid us in becoming who we are ordained to be. Your angels are sent to minister to you because you were created to inherit salvation. They are sent from God to minister to you, to strengthen you, to help you and to guide you. Hebrews 1:7 says, *"And of the angels he saith, Who maketh his angels spirits, and his ministers a flame of fire."* God made His angels as Spirit. In your interaction with angels, it is important to remember that when you work with your angels, you are working with a Spirit nature. They are ministering Spirits sent forth to them who shall be heirs of salvation. Angels are divine members of an order of heavenly beings who are superior to man in power and intelligence. By nature, angels are spiritual beings.

> *"Bless the LORD, ye his angels, that excel in strength,*
> *that do his commandments, hearkening unto the voice of*
> *his word." (Psalms 103:20)*

Everyone has a prophetic angel that is assigned to them by God. God sends your prophetic angel to give you a glimpse of your future, the future that was divinely orchestrated by the Father. When your words are in alignment with God's words, your prophetic angel takes heed to the voice of your words. Are you speaking words that reflect the truth of who God says you are, or are you speaking words that reflect what the world has labeled you to be? Are you speaking words of peace and happiness, or are you speaking words of gloom and doom? Are you speaking words of wealth and prosperity, or are you speaking words of poverty and need? Your prophetic angel is listening to your words. What are the last words you uttered that started to employ your angels and put them into action?

Principle #9

God sends your prophetic angel to give you
a glimpse of your future.

Your prophetic angel is waiting for you to give a command. Your prophetic angel is waiting in the wings, unemployed until you speak a prophetic directive. This directive will cause the angel to become attentive to your words and begin to bring into manifestation the word that God has breathed into your life. There are strategic methods that will invoke your prophetic angel. Some of these methods may seem a bit crazy and unorthodox, but believe me, they work!

METHOD 1: PROPHESY TO THE WINDS

Start consciously prophesying to the four winds and speaking prophetic directives for your angels to come from the north, the south, the east and the west. Begin to speak to your prophetic angels, invoking them to bring to you God's best. As you speak those prophetic directives into the winds, your prophetic angels will be dispatched on your behalf to summon your retrieving angels. Yes, it is a cyclical effect. Your angels work in partnership with one another. Your prophetic angels will summon your retrieving angels to go out and bring you that which the Father wants to come to pass in your life at that particular moment.

> *"Surely the Lord GOD will do nothing, but he revealeth his secret unto his servants the prophets." (Amos 3:7)*

As you prophesy to the winds in consciousness, God dispatches your angels of divine intelligence to bring you answers to your secret questions, those questions that can only be answered by God. The law of the prophet says that God will only reveal His secrets unto His servants, the prophets. As you prophesy to the winds and command prophetic intelligence to be invoked into your experience, God will send His prophetic angels to whisper in your ear the secrets that are in the King's chambers.

There is an angel at work in your situation, and because you are aware of your angels, you will begin to receive supernatural visitations. You need to start working with your angels because your angels are sent to minister to you.

Principle #10

As you prophesy to the winds in consciousness, God dispatches your angels of divine intelligence to bring you answers to your secret questions.

METHOD 2: EMPLOY YOUR ANGELS

"Behold, I send an Angel before thee, to keep thee in the way, and to bring thee into the place which I have prepared. Beware of him, and obey his voice, provoke him not; for he will not pardon your transgressions: for my name is in him." (Exodus 23:20-21)

You have to employ your angels. Some people do not experience angelic visitations because they have not put their angels to work. Your angels are waiting to hear your voice so that they can tune into your every word. They listen for your words.

When the prophet prophesies the word of the Lord to you, an angel is dispatched to bring that prophetic word to pass. The angel prepares to bring you into the place that God has prepared for you. The prophet prophesies the word of the Lord, and the angel is assigned to bring you to that place of manifestation. Oftentimes, God has to prepare us for the place that He has ordained for us because the person to whom God speaks the word is not the same person in whom He fulfills the word. How do you go from the place where He spoke the word to the place where He fulfills the word? An angel is dispatched to prepare you.

God speaks to your potential not to your experience. This is a concept that is difficult for many people to understand. There has been an angel working with you from the first day you received the word of the Lord from the prophet. Not only has that angel been working with you, that angel has been creating some divine prophetic connections. However, some of the connections cannot come to full manifestation until you come into the right consciousness. The prophet speaks the word and your prophecy angel is dispatched. But it is your responsibility to see that word through to full manifestation.

Principle #11

God speaks to your potential
not to your experience.

Dream Angels

> *"And when they were departed, behold, the angel of the*
> *Lord appeareth to Joseph in a dream, saying, Arise, and*
> *take the young child and his mother, and flee into Egypt,*

*and be thou there until I bring thee word: for Herod will
seek the young child to destroy him." (Matthew 2:13)*

Oftentimes, angels will invade your dreams to bring direction and clarity to situations or circumstances that you may be facing. The angels came to Joseph in a dream and told him to rise and take the young child and his mother, flee to Egypt and stay there until God told him otherwise. Joseph was led by angels. After he received guidance and direction from the angel of the Lord, he had to be obedient to the word. He could not doubt nor waver. He did not have time to ponder over whether that was God speaking or the devil. Joseph had to be obedient to the angel of the Lord and respond to the mandate immediately. Joseph had to take the child and go to the place that the angel directed and then stay there until his next assignment.

You are only as successful as your last act of obedience. When the angel of the Lord appears to you in a dream, it is a sign that God wants to bring divine instruction and direction to a situation or circumstance

---

Principle #12

You are only as successful as your
last act of obedience.

---

in your life. Your obedience to the angel's voice will determine your success in that particular situation. When was the last time you were obedient to your angel?

Your angels will cause you to dream yet another dream. They work in your dream world. Your angels are always at work to materialize what you visualize. If you are going to be successful in life, you must have the right vision. You must have foresight of the success that God has ordained for your life. Therefore, it is pertinent that you visualize the good that God has ordained for your life.

You have to get the right vision. You have to think the right thoughts. How do you think the right thoughts? You have to begin by eating the food of the angels, the food of the Almighty. The food of the angels is the manna that God sends from heaven: right thoughts, prosperous thoughts, healthy thoughts. Your purpose and your good incubate in your sleep. Something is growing in you while you are asleep. You are dreaming yet another dream. God will put the cure for what ails you in a dream.

> *"In a dream, in a vision of the night, when deep sleep falleth upon men, in slumberings upon the bed; then he openeth the ears of men, and sealeth their instruction. (Job 33:15-16)*

God wants to visit you in your dreams. In the Job passage, the word "night" not only signifies the physical night, but it also represents the unconscious or a place where things are not easily seen. It is only when you are dreaming that your ears are open. Dreams expose the thieves that are in your temple. They surface in your dream in what the famous psychologist, Carl Jung, calls the "collective unconscious."

In order to explore the importance of being connected to your dream world, let's look at the mythology of Dorothy in the *Wizard of Oz* and the ruby slippers. Red is a degree of power. When Dorothy stepped into the red shoes she began to spin out of control because, subconsciously, she wanted to go into a world where there were no restraints. As soon as she stepped into the ruby slippers, she began to delve into everything that was in her imagination. She explored every realm without any boundaries or limitation.

The character of Dorothy denotes a person who does not want to take responsibility for their world, their life or their spirituality. Obviously, Dorothy faced many emotional challenges in her life, and she wanted to run away from home in hopes that she could run away from those challenges. However, when she stepped into the ruby slippers, she invoked her power within, and thus she had to take responsibility for that power and use it to get herself back home.

We can see from that mystical fairytale that God visits us in our dreams and seals His instructions. Many people walk around with the power to succeed, the power to overcome the obstacles in their lives and the power to be great in God, yet they do not realize it. They have to be put into a sleep state in order for them to hear what God is saying. Dorothy went into a sleep state, and in her subconscious she was able to recognize her angels when they appeared on the scene.

Those who indulge in recreational drugs often do so to escape the natural realm in which they live. LSD, cocaine, marijuana and many other recreational drugs are the lazy man's way to meditation. God created these substances to show man that there is a way to enlightenment other than the path walked by man on earth. Getting high is easy. Getting intoxicated is easy. Staying high is the key. However, the only way to maintain that state of consciousness is to dwell in the secret place of the Most High. That is where you come into that meditative state of consciousness.

> *"And the angel of God spake unto me in a dream, saying, Jacob: And I said, Here am I. And he said, Lift up now thine eyes, and see, all the rams which leap upon the cattle are ringstraked, speckled, and grisled: for I have seen all that Laban doeth unto thee. I am the God of Bethel, where thou anointedst the pillar, and where thou vowedst a vow unto me: now arise, get thee out from this land, and return unto the land of thy kindred."* (Genesis 31:11-13)

God seals your instructions in the sleep state. Your angels are working in your dreams. Your mind is like a television screen. Dreams are a series of thoughts that appear to you in images on the screen of your mind. Some people remember their dreams and others forget their dreams. Some people wish they could turn the channel because they don't want to work through particular areas of their lives.

Ask not what is divine. God blossoms from the branches. You may think that the branch is different from the blossom, but it is all the same. Although you are in a physical body, you decide when you go to sleep. You decide what dreams you will have. It is God blossoming out of the branches. So, if you are born of God, God blossomed in thee. How can you be an offspring of God, created in His image and His likeness and not be God? Deep calleth unto deep. Many people believe that God is up in the sky. However, wherever you are, there God is also, because God dwells within you and me. "I and my Father are one." Even if we were to pray to a God in the sky, He is here, here, here, here and here!

Principle #13

How can you be an offspring of God, created in
His image and His likeness and not be God?

2

The Power of Your Prophetic Angels

God's Prophetic Servants (GPS)

> *"And the angel of the LORD found her by a fountain of water in the wilderness, by the fountain in the way to Shur." And he said, Hagar, Sarai's maid, whence camest thou? and whither wilt thou go? And she said, I flee from the face of my mistress Sarai. And the angel of the LORD said unto her, Return to thy mistress, and submit thyself under her hands." (Genesis 16:7-9)*

The first time angels are mentioned in scripture is in Genesis 16:7. The scripture says, *"And the angel of the Lord found her..."* The angels are in search of you. The law of first mention supports this interpretation throughout the scriptures. The angels are your GPS system (God's Prophetic Servants). It doesn't matter where you are in the universe;

your angels know exactly where you are and can navigate you to where you need to be.

Your angels will give you direction. They will let you know when you are off center or out of alignment and when you need to get back to your rightful place. Even when your life is in chaos and your actions cause you to act in ways that seem out of order, your angels will summon you to return and submit to God's purpose. Your angels are always pointing you back to the authority to which you should be connected.

Principle #14

Your angels have multiplying power.

Notice that in Genesis 16:10, the angel of the Lord said, *"I will multiply thy seed exceedingly."* Say with me, "My angel is multiplying me." Not only are your angels sent to find you and navigate you to where you need to be in God, but they are also assigned to multiply that which is important to you. Notice here, the angel is doing the multiplying. We have been trained to think that God does the multiplying, but that is not what the scripture says. The scripture says that the angel said, "I will multiply you." Your angels have multiplying power. In today's failing economy, you should be working with your personal prophetic angel to guarantee that multiplication. Keep in mind that your prophetic angel is at work on your behalf right now.

"And the angel of the LORD said unto her, Behold, thou art with child and shalt bear a son, and shalt call his name Ishmael; because the LORD hath heard thy affliction." (Genesis:16:11)

Repeat after me, "I am with child." The enemy has tried to convince you that you are barren, but the Spirit of the Lord wants you to receive the message that today you are with child. You are pregnant with purpose, vision, dreams, thoughts and ideas that are designed to multiply and bring you into the fullness of all that God has ordained for your life. But you have to believe within yourself that you are with child. Never confess what you don't have. God has dispatched His angels in your life to bring divine increase.

Understand that, regardless of where you are in life, your angels will find you. You cannot hide from God or His angels. Therefore, every time trouble shows up, your "GPS system" **(God's Prophetic Servant)** sounds an alarm indicating that you need supernatural intervention from God. Just like in the movies when the superhero shows up to save the city from the villain, you can count on your angels to show up and save you from the traps and pitfalls of the enemy.

Guard, Guide and Direct

"When I consider thy heavens, the work of thy fingers, the moon and the stars, which thou hast ordained; What is man, that thou art mindful of him? and the son of man, that thou visitest him? For thou hast made him a little lower than the angels, and hast crowned him with glory and honour. Thou madest him to have dominion over the

works of thy hands; thou hast put all things under his feet:" (Psalms 8:3-6)

Your angels have an office and an assignment, which is to guard, guide and direct your life. You must allow your angels the high and holy privilege of carrying out their pre-ordained assignment from God.

Consider the example of David. David considered the heavens. It can be inferred from the scriptures that before David did anything he consulted with the heavens. He even identified which heaven he was consulting with: the work of God's fingers, the moon and the stars. The heavens encompass the handwriting of God in the sky. David was working with astrology, the logos or the speech of the astros (the speech of the stars). David knew the heavens were declaring the glory of God. He wanted to establish that the heavens were not the work of Satan, but the work of the hand of God. In other words, God used his fingers to screw the light bulbs into the universe—Venus, Jupiter, Saturn, Mars, Mercury, the Sun, the Moon. It was all the work of God's fingers, the handiwork of God.

The influence of the heavens in the work of God is evident in that it was during the New Moon that the people would come and consult the prophet. In scripture, when the woman's child had died and she told her husband that she was going to see the prophet, her husband responded that it was neither New Moon nor Sabbath. The New Moon was considered just as holy as the Sabbath was in Israel.

Verse 5 says, *"For thou hast made him a little lower than the angels, and hast crowned him with glory and honour."* In the Hebrew, it translates as "a little lower than Elohim." I have good news for you. The Lord made Man higher than the angels, but a little lower than God. As a spiritual being made a little lower than God Himself, you can gain dominion over your world and completely cast out and dissolve negative experiences in your life. That is why angels are sent to serve you. Clearly, your prophetic angels carry great power. When you start to understand who you are and how you were created, you will utilize that power to dissolve the negative experiences in your life.

> *"I formed the light and created darkness. I make peace and create evil. I, the Lord, do all these things."* *(Isaiah 45:7)*

Everything begins in your God-self, whether good, bad or indifferent. Believe it or not, all things have their beginning in you. The moment you discover who He is, you will recognize who you are. There is no power outside of God. To understand the existence of negative experiences, it is imperative to clarify the origin of evil. Light allows you to see on this real (visible, three-dimensional) plane, but darkness represents the unseen realm, the place where creation occurs. God created evil. So, whatever evil exists, the God-in-you created it. God only serves to us what we give to Him. Your outward experiences are only a manifestation of what is taking place inside of you. The universe is a mirror of who you are. The world will always mirror you. Therefore, you create the world in which you live. Whether a world of lack or a world of prosperity, you create that world.

Principle #15

Everything begins in your God-self,
whether good, bad or indifferent.

Your Guardian Angels

You have guardian angels protecting you at all times. Because God is guarding and protecting you, your guardian angels are present in your life to help aid and assist you. God sees through those seasons of life that you might need help and assistance. Your guardian angels watch over and protect you not with the eyes, but with thought in Spirit, through consciousness.

The word "protect" is defined as, "to shield from injury, danger or loss." You have a protecting angel. Your angel shields and protects you from hurt, harm and danger. Your guardian angels act as your shield of protection. Not only are your guardian angels shielding you, but your guardian angels are protecting you from all loss and danger. Because you have angels at work on your behalf, nothing can be lost in the universe. Could it be that something gets lost only to provoke you to use your angels to help you find it? The real question is, "Are you working with your angel?"

Principle #16

Your guardian angels act as your shield of protection.

When things begin to take place in your life, it is only for you to begin to recognize and to know that you are not alone. You have help on the other side, outside of this physical sphere. Your angels never sleep nor slumber. Your angels are waiting for directions from you, just standing, waiting at attention. Whenever you call on your angels, they are there to respond to your request. Your angels are trying to open your eyes so you can see something that you do not yet see.

The Angel of God's Presence

> *"There shall no evil befall thee, neither shall any plague come nigh thy dwelling. For he shall give his angels charge over thee, to keep thee in all thy ways."* *(Psalm 91:10-11)*

The ancient mystics believed that the angel of God's presence is a miracle-working presence that is available to every man. That is to say that God has placed His angels of protection all around us to guide and protect us when we need them. They also believed that every person has an angel of higher self. Your angels are in your life to usher you into the place of prosperity, a place that God has prepared for you. The place is already prepared. The good news is you do not have to prepare the way for yourself. It is already prepared for you whenever you are ready to manifest it in your experience.

The angels have been assigned to do all the work for you. All you have to do is be obedient and move forward. Your willingness and obedience will cause your angels to act in accordance to their assignment and bring prosperity to you. Isaiah 1:19 says, *"If ye be willing and obedient, ye shall eat the good of the land."* Your angel of prosperity wants you to eat the good of the land. He goes before you to prepare the way. Your angel goes before you to annihilate the enemies that might be in the way. Your angels want to meet your enemy before your enemy meets you. God commanded your angels to have charge over you so that you are safe in everything that you do. It feels good to feel kept.

Principle #17

Your willingness and obedience will cause
your angels to move in their assignment
and bring prosperity to you.

Tapping Into Your Angel Power

Within you lies a power to do, to be and to have all that God has designed for your life. Once you tap into this power, it becomes a steady pressure, demanding attention and expression in your life. That power can be described as "God within." Most people are only familiar with the universal God or the God outside of themselves. Many pray to a God in the sky, somewhere out there in the distance. But the true, manifested presence of God lives inside each of us. God is evenly present everywhere. Once you affirm that the presence of God lives within you and that there is only one presence, you are able to tap into that power and walk into the divine manifestation of God.

The God-Self only operates when you search within. If you look for a God outside of you, you will be guilty of dwelling in idolatry. Scripture says, "I am God and beside me there is no other." You must get rid of the mindset of another god or you will not walk in true victory, nor will you experience prosperity. The moment you realize that God is your reality, then, you will express God as reality. Rest in your reality, and realize that real and material are not the same. God comes to reveal Himself so that you can operate on earth in your God-Self.

Principle #18

The God-Self only operates
when you go within.

"I am crucified with Christ: nevertheless I live; yet not
I, but Christ liveth in me: and the life which I now live in

the flesh I live by the faith of the Son of God, who loved
me, and gave himself for me. (Galatians 2:20)

You are only as powerful as the realization of the I Am within you. Paul said, "I am crucified with Christ: nevertheless I live; yet not I, but Christ liveth in me." It is no longer the "I" (the ego), but it is only Christ that is living in me. Therefore, my "me" is God. This brings us to a revelation of accountability (your reality is your creation, not someone else's). There is the "I" who is the real self or the individual, and there is the "me" who is attached to and belongs to the "I", the personality.

"And if Christ be in you, the body is dead because of sin;
but the Spirit is life because of righteousness. But if the
Spirit of him that raised up Jesus from the dead dwell in
you, he that raised up Christ from the dead shall also
quicken your mortal bodies by his Spirit that dwelleth in
you." (Romans 8:10-11)

The real you is Spirit. You are Spirit having a human experience. The Spirit of God is dwelling in you. Every one of us is playing a part in the great play of life. We come to earth with a purpose to bring into manifestation. What resides in us are all of the components of the part we are to play. But depending on our mindset, we can alter our parts. We can play the beggar or we can play the rich man. We can play sickness or we can play divine health. We can play any part we choose. The question is; which part are you playing?

Our personality is just a mask. Every one of us is hiding behind a mask. Yet the real self, the "I", that part of which you are conscious when you say "I Am," is the real essential power. Many of us do not know how powerful we are, because sometimes we get lost behind our masks. Sometimes you take to heart what people say about your mask. However, you have to rise up beyond your mask. You have to start declaring, "I am rich," because "I Am" (your God-Self) is rich. You have to declare, "I am healed," because "I Am" is whole. You have to declare, "I am above and not beneath," because "I Am" is the head and not the tail, above and not beneath. You have to get in touch with the real you, the real self that is behind the mask.

Everything is waiting for you to suggest it to be so, and then use your God-power to bring it into full manifestation. Once you have a certainty, the power to believe against all odds, you will start to see victory in your life. That is the victory that Jesus wants you to demonstrate. It comes from an energy held within you. When you start to walk in that victory, you are going to start to see some things that are going to bring you into new territory.

Principle #19

The real you is spirit.

3

Look Around You!

"Then spake Haggai the LORD's messenger in the LORD's message unto the people, saying, I am with you, saith the LORD." (Haggai 1:13)

Steadfast Prayer

> *"And Jacob was left alone; and there wrestled a man with him until the breaking of the day. And when he saw that he prevailed not against him, he touched the hollow of his thigh; and the hollow of Jacob's thigh was out of joint, as he wrestled with him. And he said, Let me go, for the day breaketh. And he said, I will not let thee go, except thou bless me." (Genesis 32:24-26)*

You have an angel on assignment. Although a demon is constantly deceived by other demons, an angel can never be deceived by a demon. Therefore, the angel of God's presence counsels you wisely. The angel will never be led astray by evil deception. You are always given wise counsel when you work with your angels. They are leading you and directing your thoughts in action and in harmony, in peace and poise, in love and in cooperation. As you begin to work with your angels, your angels are going to start working with you, in you and through you. However, to enjoy the full benefits of working with your angels, you must be steadfast in prayer and determined not to let your angels go until they bless you.

Jacob wrestled all night with the angel, praying the angel would not leave him until he received his blessing. Similarly, we must be persistent in prayer. The Bible says we must pray without ceasing. (1 Thessalonians 5:17) Jesus said that man ought to always pray and not faint. (Luke 18:1) The word "always" is the operative word in the scripture. You have to always pray and never tire. Pray in your upper room, in solitude. The prayers that we pray in secret are the prayers that are answered openly. Secret prayers bring open blessings.

Principle #20

Secret prayers bring open blessings.

What if I told you that your angels are with you throughout eternity, could you buy that? What if I told you that your angels were with you before God breathed you into this realm, could you buy that? What if I told you that the angels that are with you now are your angels of eternity past, which are the same angels of your eternity future? Your angels have been with you from the beginning. The angel of God's presence does not stop working with you when you cease on earth. Once you have been touched by an angel, that touch stays with you for eternity.

"Be still, and know that I am God…" (Psalm 46:10)

Prayer in the right direction has the power to overcome any obstacle, challenge, situation or problem. Our prayers must be strategic, methodical and scientific. Scientific prayer requires us to isolate ourselves and still our bodies, our Minds and our Spirits. We should not process any thoughts or conjure up words to say. Scientific prayer only requires that we be still and know. Did you know that your every waking thought, your every prayer establishes a goal? Our lives are made up of a series of goals. Goals are as natural as breathing. What goals have you established? God has sent you an angel to assist you in accomplishing your goals.

Principle #21

Scientific prayer only requires that
we be still and know.

The Wrestling Match

Jacob was left alone and there wrestled with a man. It wasn't a little baby with an arrow. It wasn't one of Aphrodite's children. It was not Cupid. He wrestled with a man. Jacob recognized the angel in that man was determined not to let go of him. He realized that his blessing rested within the wrestling. The wrestling match with his angel represented Jacob wrestling with his thoughts. Had he not overcome or seized his thoughts, he would not have received the blessing. His Spirit man knew that there was a blessing there and he could not let go. He was determined to stay there until the blessings were manifested.

In the midst of the wrestling, Jacob's thigh went out of joint. He wrestled with the angel until it changed his walk. He did not stop wrestling with the angel to tend to his injured leg. He didn't reach for the problem or the pain. He did not focus on the negative and use it as an excuse to surrender. Instead, he continued to wrestle with the angel and kept wrestling to hold on to his blessing.

You cannot allow life's circumstances and issues to stop you from reaching your goals and seeing the manifestation of God's promises in your life. You have to wrestle beyond the pain. The secret of winners is they never quit, and the secret of quitters is they never win. What are you willing to wrestle?

Jacob was left alone that night. Darkness or night is one of the greatest Biblical symbols, and is a metaphor for trouble and limitation. Struggle always comes in the dark night of the soul, in blackness and despair. Jacob wrestled with his angel until the breaking of day. When the dark hour comes and we have to struggle seemingly alone, that is the time when we will experience our closest connection with God and take our greatest step forward. But, this will only happen if we hold fast to the truth, if we will wrestle with our idea of God. You have to hold on to your thoughts until they are ready to break into day. You may wrestle tonight, but only so that you can break into the substance of a new day.

Principle #22

You have to wrestle beyond your pain.

Sent to Deliver

> *"Then Nebuchadnezzar spake, and said, Blessed be the God of Shadrach, Meshach, and Abednego, who hath sent his angel, and delivered his servants that trusted in him, and have changed the king's word, and yielded their bodies, that they might not serve nor worship any god, except their own God." (Daniel 3:28)*

Your angels are sent to deliver you and assist you so that you will worship no other god but the true and living God. Your angels are here to make sure you are not ashamed. You cannot expect the enemy to give you the tools to succeed. You cannot run to freedom in "Pharaoh's chariot." "Pharaoh" is not going to provide the car fare for you to be free, nor is he going to give you a freedom pass. Your angels act as your mediators, pointing you in the direction that God would have you go in a particular season of your life.

Sometimes God wants to see how long you can wrestle with your thoughts until you prevail. How you wrestle in your night season will determine what is revealed in the day. You must be persistent until you end up with the blessing.

$\mathcal{P}rinciple$ #23

Your angels are sent to deliver you and assist you so that you will worship no other god but the true and living God.

Angels Are Always Around You

> *"And there came two angels to Sodom at even; and Lot sat in the gate of Sodom: and Lot seeing them rose up to meet them; and he bowed himself with his face toward the ground." (Genesis 19:1)*

Angels are always around us. However, we must become angel conscious so that we can start seeing the manifestation of God in our experience. God is lifting you up so that you can see your angelic hosts that are participating in the affairs of your life. The angel of divine presence is with you. Just look up and you will see that there is an angel already fighting for you. There is a divine hedge of protection around you.

> *"And it came to pass, when Joshua was by Jericho, that he lifted up his eyes and looked, and, behold, there stood a man over against him with his sword drawn in his hand: and Joshua went unto him, and said unto him, Art thou for us, or for our adversaries? And he said, Nay; but as captain of the host of the LORD am I now come. And Joshua fell on his face to the earth, and did worship, and said unto him, What saith my Lord unto his servant? And the captain of the LORD's host said unto Joshua, Loose thy shoe from off thy foot; for the place whereon thou standest is holy. And Joshua did so."* (Joshua 5:13-15)

There is an angel that is always standing beside you with his sword drawn, ready to protect you from anything that tries to hinder the power and the greatness inside of you. Your angel is at work. You have a captain of the Lord's hosts that is at work within you. Therefore, every place you step on is holy.

> *Let's enter into a prophetic act right at this moment. Begin to slip your feet out of your shoes and sanctify this time as holy. Let's declare the place where our feet rest as holy ground.*

Principle #24

We must become angel conscious so that
we can start seeing the manifestation
of God in our experience.

The angel of the Lord will bring forth the manifestation of God's divine presence. Something good is getting ready to happen for you. The place where you are standing right now is holy. The atmosphere is holy. God is putting you in a place of uncommon favor and you have the ability to summon your angels.

> *"And Jesus said unto him, 'Friend, wherefore art thou come?' Then came they, and laid hands on Jesus and took him. And, behold, one of them which were with Jesus stretched out his hand, and drew his sword, and struck a servant of the high priest's, and smote off his ear. Then said Jesus unto him, 'Put up again thy sword into his place: for all they that take the sword shall perish with the sword. Thinkest thou that I cannot now pray to my Father, and he shall presently give me more than twelve legions of angels?'" (Matthew 26:50-53)*

Did you know that you have more than 12 legions of angels working on your behalf? Matthew 26:53 in the Amplified Bible says, *"Do you suppose that I cannot appeal to My Father, and He will immediately provide Me with more than twelve legions [more than 80,000] of angels"?* Twelve legions of angels is equivalent to 80,000. You have 80,000 angels at your disposal. Remember, angels come in the guise of man. Many of us have men working for us of whom we are not aware.

Jesus came not to reveal Himself, but He came to reveal YOU. If you knew how powerful you looked in the Spirit world, you would never hold your head down another day in your life. Imagine! You have tens of thousands of angels working on your behalf! The body of Christ should never be in a state of want. We should put our angels to work. There should be abundance and overflow in our midst at all times because we have more than 80,000 angels working on our behalf. Can you imagine how bored your angels have been because you have kept them unemployed? They have been waiting for you to give them instruction so that they can begin to materialize in the natural world what God has already breathed for you in Spirit.

Principle #25

You have 80,000 angels at your disposal.

The Angel of Divine Increase

> *"And it came to pass that night, that the angel of the LORD went out, and smote in the camp of the Assyrians an hundred fourscore and five thousand: and when they arose early in the morning, behold, they were all dead corpses." (2 Kings 19:35)*

You have an angel that is assigned to go out on your behalf to slay your enemies. It is vital that you ready yourself because there is an angel of divine increase that is assigned to bless your life. Your angel of divine increase is your prophetic messenger sent on assignment by God to unlock doors of health, wealth, prosperity, peace, love and joy. Your angel of divine increase is at work to bring you into the good that God intends for you, and to guard you from your enemies. Whatever situation is standing in your way, know that your angel of divine increase is going to take out 185,000 of your enemies by morning.

Your angels are at work as Spirit. Psalms 104:4 says, *"Who maketh his angels spirits; his ministers a flaming fire."* The New International Version says, *"He makes wind his messenger, a flame of fire his servant."* The prophet is the servant of God, who brings the word of God with fire. What does that mean? The prophet comes to burn up those things that don't belong and might stand in the way of your prosperity. The angels are spirits and minister a flame of fire. There is a heavenly intelligence that operates when God employs them to carry on His government for the world.

$\mathcal{P}rinciple$ #26

Your angels are at work as Spirit.

Resting in the Stillness

> *"Come unto me all ye that labor and are heavy laden and I will give you rest. Take my yoke upon you and learn from me for I am meek and lowly in heart and ye shall find rest for your souls." (Matthew 11:28-29)*

Rest is given to those that come to God. There is rest in your coming. When you come to God, God will come to you. God meets Himself in you. Because the presence and the power of God dwell in you, whatever is contrary to your state of being is only temporary. Therefore, you must learn to separate yourself from everything that contradicts the nature of your being. You only speak to those who are in sync with your nature. Sometimes we want to hold on to who we are. Sometimes we want to hold on to what we're doing. But we have to let go of the self. Letting go of the self becomes key to acting and operating in life.

Creativity is generated in a place of peace. You should never try to produce because you are under pressure to do so. You must learn how to center yourself so that you can generate from the center of who you are. The word "relax" means to loosen and to release. When you practice the prayer of relaxation you learn how to loosen and release your problems so that they can be resolved. If it is not loosened and released through the law of relaxation then there is no resolution in the future for it. The prayer of relaxation brings you to a point where you can loosen and release. Once you do that you are in a meditative state where you can create and resolve.

> *"Finally, brethren, whatsoever things are true, whatsoever things are honest, whatsoever things are just, whatsoever things are pure, whatsoever things are lovely, whatsoever things are of good report; if there be any virtue, and if there be any praise, think on these things." (Philippians 4:8)*

Principle #27

Creativity is generated in a place of peace.

You have to be careful of the thoughts that you think and that on which you ponder. The Bible says think on those things which are lovely. Think on those things which are true. Think on those things which are honest. Think on those things which are pure. None of those things are supposed to be stressful. If it's lovely, it's peaceful. If you were violated, that is not lovely; do not think on it. God wants your mind on things that bring peace. Isaiah 26:3 says, *"I will keep you in perfect peace if your mind is stayed on me."* The mind has to be stayed, steadied in peace.

Silence is the place of creation. It is the place where you ready yourself. Your emergency does not move God. Your disaster does not hurry God. Your need does not get God to move on your behalf. Your desperation does not cause God to act. This might be painful, but you have to be still and know that God has everything under control. Stillness readies the Mind to receive the movement of God in you. Stillness readies the Spirit for the movement of God in you. All things will be so when the Mind is ready.

You cannot find His presence in the noise. That's why the prophet found God in the still, small voice. You can't hear God in the noise unless you can find the stillness in the center of the noise. Whatever you are lacking, it is because you haven't found the stillness in you. There is a place in the eye of the storm where it is safe. In the center there is safety. You have to get into the center of who you are. The center of your being brings you into the safety of God.

When we look at the Lord's Supper, the disciples were in a relaxed position. As a matter of fact, one of the disciples had his head on Jesus' breast. So, they were leaning and relaxing. In the Greek culture, when the people would pontificate, they would sit on the porch in a relaxed position, eating grapes and receiving revelation. When you are in a relaxed state, knowledge flows. When you are protecting ideas and ideologies about yourself, you are in attack mode. This posture blocks new concepts and ideas. But, when you relax and are at peace, then all the universe will be at peace with you. Life meets you the way you meet life.

God will not speak in the heat of your circumstances. He only talks in the "cool" of your day. Once the mind is in that state of relaxation, that's when we do our programming. That is the cool of your day, the cooling down period where you can relax and do your spiritual work in your sleep state of consciousness. You cannot relax in the heat. You can't hear God in the heat. We must know how to enter into the silence. Don't take offense when somebody tells you to be silent. Let God speak. When you let God speak within you, He will start talking through you. That is entering the divine silence.

Principle #28

Life meets you the way you meet life.

The manifestation of things can only come about when one comes into that relaxed state of prayer. You cannot manifest in turmoil. That's why the enemy of your soul tries to get your body up in arms. If you are not at rest, God doesn't speak. He doesn't speak in the fire; his voice is not found in the wind; his voice is not even found in an earthquake. He is not even in the storm that is going on around you. But He is in the still, small voice. Sometimes you have to move away from the elements and take a silent bath. Bathe in silence, a period when you are baptizing yourself, when you hear nothing outside of you. Allow your mind to close off all thoughts and center yourself. Find the still place and there you will find God.

Principle #29

Life meets you the way you meet life.

4

Shadow Work

The Struggle Within

> *"But the children struggled together within her; and she said, "If all is well, why am I like this?" So she went to inquire of the LORD." (Genesis 25:22)*

"To struggle" means "to make strenuous or violent efforts in the face of difficulty or opposition." Struggle can have a major significance in your life. Oftentimes, struggle will come when God is trying to manifest Himself in your life. Tension, struggle and challenges are not bad. The question is what do we do and where do we go when the struggles begin to surface in our lives.

Opposition is a catalyst for growth. Jesus came to earth and created the greatest amount of tension, then redeemed it and brought closure again. Opposition! You can never be found unless you were once lost. Notice Jesus did not rejoice over the sheep that were good in the sheepfold. He only rejoiced over the sheep that created opposition and then came back into the sheepfold. The prodigal son created opposition. He rebelled and left his father's house, only to return. His father rejoiced in his return and put a ring on his finger. Opposition!

In order to know God, you have to resign to your sense of awareness of God. In order to be saved, you have to first be lost. This is the mystery of iniquity. So, why does God allow tension in your life? In an astrological chart, if a person's chart denotes all good aspects and no negatives, it means that they will not experience challenges in their life. This person is referred to as a "kindergarten soul." The kindergarten soul will never grow because it never has to fight against opposition and resistance. It will never grow because it never has any resistance to move against.

Principle #30

Opposition is a catalyst for growth.

During my trip to Greece, I went mountain climbing, a physical activity that helped me gain a better perspective on the importance of opposition and resistance in our natural lives. We climbed some vast mountains, oftentimes climbing so high that we were above the clouds. For the first time in my life, I was celebrating resistance. As we climbed, I was looking for the stones that were stumbling blocks to use them as footing to help me reach the next height. Opposition! If the terrain were smooth as we climbed the mountain, I would have never made it to the top.

The stumbling blocks in your life are there so that you can use them to catapult you to your success. It is the resistance and opposition that give you that traction that you need to move to the next level in life.

Seeds also help us visualize this principle. All seeds look for resistance. A seed is placed into the ground and dirt is piled on top of it. The seed celebrates the resistance of the dirt packed over it. Its only reward for living is its ability to grow beyond the dirt that is packed on top of it. Opposition!

> *"The stone that the builders rejected has become the chief cornerstone." (Mark 12:10)*

Here is a master key. The greater your rejection, the greater your anointing. You are not anointed until you are rejected. Your rejection is designed to protect your anointing. Until you celebrate opposition, you will not experience growth in your life. The fact that you have experienced poverty is a sign that you are a candidate for prosperity. However, many have stayed under the dirt and never gave themselves permission to rise up against the resistance.

Principle #31

The greater your rejection, the greater your anointing.

Change cannot come until your pain becomes larger than the fear of change. You have to become larger than your pain to provoke change. Some people have signed up for "pain management" class. Wrong class! In medicine, when the doctors have exhausted all of their options for treatment and have given up hope, they often tell the patient, "All we can do for you is to help manage your pain." Well, in life, your pain is not to be managed. Your pain is not to be dulled. Your pain is designed to provoke change.

Pain is a signal that something is out of place. Some people have learned to accept their pain instead of making the decision to change and eradicate the pain. If someone puts your arm behind your back and keeps lifting it, what are you going to feel? Pain. Why are you going to feel pain when your arm is behind your back? Because your arm does not belong there. Many people are in economic and financial pain. Why? Because they just don't belong there!

Inquire of the Lord

> *"Now there was a man of Benjamin, whose name was Kish, the son of Abiel, the son of Zeror, the son of*

Bechorath, the son of Aphiah, a Benjamite, a mighty man of power. And he had a son, whose name was Saul, a choice young man, and a goodly: and there was not among the children of Israel a goodlier person than he: from his shoulders and upward he was higher than any of the people." (1 Samuel 9:1-2)

Saul was a Benjamite. "Benjamin" means "son of my right hand." Benjamin was the brother, possibly the full brother, of Joseph. Joseph was put in prison by his brothers. Joseph's father gave him a coat of many colors. Esoterically, that means that Joseph had a greater imagination than the rest of his brothers. He was multifaceted, multi-talented. You can't be a good prophet without imagination. Imagination is creation. You can't manifest without imagination. So, whenever God anoints a man or a woman, He gives them the ability to imagine the possibilities of what can be.

It does not take faith to see what you are in the present. It takes faith to see your potential in God. It is difficult for me to see objectively. If you show me a seed, I see an apple orchard. If you show me your last dollar, I see an account that the FDIC cannot insure. Show me a man, I see a nation. Show me a person that is sick, I see someone on their way to experiencing a miracle. Show me someone who is downtrodden, I see a resurrected individual coming out of the sod of life. When the prophet's eyes are on your situation, it is difficult to explain the miraculous works that will assist you in your transition.

You do have angels working with you, but in the midst you will have to contend with the struggle; struggle creates tension. Why the tension? Why the struggle? Why the opposition? Opposition shows up for a reason. You have to ask yourself, "What is the life lesson that I am supposed to learn?" You might as well learn it now so that you do not have to repeat it.

Principle #32

You can't manifest without imagination.

"And the asses of Kish, Saul's father, were lost; and Kish said to Saul his son, Take now one of the servants with thee, and arise, go seek the asses. And he passed through mount Ephraim, and passed through the land of Shalisha, but they found them not: then they passed through the land of Shalim, and there they were not: and he passed through the land of the Benjamites, but they found them not." (1 Samuel 9:3-4)

Kish discovered that his asses were lost, which caused the tension to increase. The tension moved him into action. There is a reason for the tension. There is a reason for the opposition. People always seek the prophet when there is tension and opposition in their lives. When everything is going well, the prophet is usually never sought. People seek after the prophet when life throws a question in their situation. Most people come to the prophet when they are at the last stop in life. Although everyone around you may appear as if they have it together, they probably do not. Tension is necessary because we are taught to "fake it until you make it."

> "And when they were come to the land of Zuph, Saul said to his servant that was with him, Come, and let us return; lest my father leave caring for the asses, and take thought for us. And he said unto him, Behold now, there is in this city a man of God, and he is an honourable man; all that he saith cometh surely to pass: now let us go thither; peradventure he can shew us our way that we should go." (1 Samuel 9:4-6)

Right in the midst of the confusion, they remembered that there was a man of God in the city. In the midst of confusion and calamity, people will seek the prophet for answers. In this hour of economic unrest and financial turmoil, the prophets are in demand. Companies that have been around for a hundred years are threatening to collapse. We would have never thought a year ago that Merrill Lynch would close its doors. Major businesses and institutions are folding so quickly I am having a hard time even keeping up with who is still with us and who is gone. When it is time for transition, God allows that which is secure to collapse underneath us. Transition will always look like death because change is on the horizon.

$\mathcal{P}rinciple$ #33

In the midst of confusion and calamity, people will seek the prophet for answers.

When Rebecca inquired of the Lord because of the struggle that was in her womb, she pressed her way to find a prophet. Even if she were living in today's times, she would still need to inquire of a prophet. A sonogram could tell her she was carrying twins, but it could not tell her the quality of the twins. The prophet, however, could tell her the destiny of the twins. Only the prophet can tell you the destiny of the relationship.

I prophesied to a woman a few years ago concerning healing in her body. At the time she had a tumor in her stomach and was seeking a healing miracle from God. The prophetic word was that she would conceive a child. She said, "I came for a situation with a tumor and the word comes about a baby? What is going on here?" The woman was past the age where she could even get pregnant. She did conceive and the baby moved the tumor.

You may inquire of the prophet for direction, but the word of prophecy will not always make sense. God will put you in a relationship that does not make sense or cause you to embrace something that doesn't make any sense, because He has a destiny that is bigger than your present day picture. I flow in what does not make sense, because when it is God, He will always confirm His word with signs, wonders and miracles.

There's a War Going On

"And the LORD said unto her, Two nations are in thy womb, and two manner of people shall be separated from thy bowels; and the one people shall be stronger than the other people; and the elder shall serve the younger." (Genesis 25:23)

There was a struggle happening in Rebecca's womb. There were two nations within her. Rebecca was given a prophecy while all of this was something going. God spoke a word that essentially said, "One nation is going to have mastery over the other," and Rebecca never forgot what God had told her.

Oftentimes, we struggle because we are about to give birth to something that is uncommon. I have been carrying uncommon twins within me most of my life, but I am learning to rejoice. Not only does it come with the territory, but the outcome always powerful. Learn to celebrate opposition. Learn to welcome opposition. When people talk negatively about me, I know that I am on the right track. It comes with the office.

Your prophecy angel whispered in the ears of your parents the destiny that God created for you. There is a prophetic word that was given to you that is hovering over your life waiting for manifestation. You are pregnant with something great. The prophet finds his way into your life during a season of crises and helps interpret and translate the mind of God for your situation.

Rebecca never forgot the prophecy that she received from God. From the moment she heard the prophetic word, she was always giving birth to her prophecy. The prophetic word is like your lifeline. It is imperative that you do not break your prophetic connection because your prophecy angel has divine words of instruction and revelation that will change your mind about what you see in the natural and place your focus on Spirit. Breaking your prophetic connection is like losing your sight. God stirs up opposition to see how you can handle it. Your prophetic connection is like your spiritual umbilical cord, without it there would be no real life.

The moon is more visible when it is in opposition to the sun. You can't see too much when the moon is under the sun's beam. A planet is not that powerful when it is under the sun's beam. It becomes powerful when it is furthest away from the sun. The opposition becomes stronger because you're able to see two individual points. When it is a new moon, it is dark and you are unable to see. It is only when there is opposition that you can truly see.

Principle #34

Your prophetic connection is like
your spiritual umbilical cord.

"Surely God will do nothing unless he first revealeth his secrets to his servants, the prophets." (Amos 3:7)

It is most important that you maintain your prophetic connection. Yes, with God you are going to be established; but if you believe His prophet, you are going to prosper. If you plan on prospering, there must be a prophet in your life prophesying to your potential, waking up your life, putting life back into your existence and reviving the dead things that God wants alive.

In the midst of a failing economy, foreclosures, unemployment, churches suffering, pastors suffering, leaders suffering, business owners suffering, people need the prophetic word. Right in the midst of a situation that is drying up, you need the prophetic word in your life to remind you of what God breathed into you from the foundation of the world. You need a prophet in your life, a prophet in your ear, a prophet calling your house. You need the prophet to interfere with the limitation and lack and point you in the direction of infinite supply. Sometimes it is even a matter of life or death. When I look at the word "intercession" I see the word "intercept." Some people need prophetic interception because they need some things blocked from their lives. Are you ready for a prophetic interception?

Opposition could be the full throw of a revelation that is coming into play. Why has there been tension created in your life? Because God wants you to see something about your life. You are going to create tension once you find your difference. No one gets rewarded for sameness, but you get rewarded for your difference. Heaven does not reward copies. Heaven only rewards uniqueness. Say with me, "Thank God for the angels who are at work in my life."

Principle #35

Heaven only rewards uniqueness.

The Crossing Principle

Rebecca never forgot the prophetic word spoken to her. She did everything in her power to help Jacob because of the prophetic word that she received that the elder shall serve the younger. Jacob, the second of the twins to be born, was ordained to supplant his brother Esau as the family patriarch. According to tradition, as the eldest male, Esau was supposed to be the patriarch of the family. He was the chosen one to be the spiritual authority. He was supposed to maintain the social unit of the family. Tradition would say that the oldest son would succeed the father. But because of a prophecy Rebecca heard, God would cross his hands and Jacob would take the place of Esau.

As soon as Jacob and Esau were born, it was apparent that there were two different individuals coming out of the womb. Esau had a hairy appearance, and Jacob was smooth skinned, suggesting they had opposite natures. Even though they had the same parents, they had different destinies. The same applies to all siblings. Esau was a man of the outdoors. He was physically robust and active, a sort of super-masculine character. Yet he thought in a literal, down-to-earth way, like his father, and was concerned with the environment, having a "what's for dinner" mentality. Inevitably, he became his father's favorite. However, just because someone is the father's favorite, that does not mean they are God's choice. A moment was coming when there would be a transfer.

Whenever God crosses his hands concerning an individual, it is because he has a destiny plan in mind. You may be considered the "black sheep" of your family. You may have been in last place for most of your life. You may be in a dilemma where it appears that your future is uncertain. However, God is crossing His hands and putting you in first place. God has a prophecy angel on assignment working for you.

Esau seemed to have been the extrovert, while Jacob was, seemingly, the introvert. While one had to go outside to get what he needed, the other had to discover it from within. Sometimes you are thrown into depression so that you can go within and retrieve the treasure that is going to bless you and bring you forth and raise your status on the out-side. There is a prophetic word that is hanging over your life that is about to fulfill itself at an opportune time. God is about to showcase the promise he has made unto you.

God has crossed his hands for many of you reading this book right now. You could not get to a prophet unless you were in a crossed up sit-uation and people have written you off. The only reason you could respond to the prophet is because something leaped in the womb of your spirit and caused you to connect.

You may have been getting your resources like Esau, going outside, when God wants you to go within. Some people are worried about being laid off from their jobs—going outside instead of going within. Some people are worried about losing their homes—going outside instead of going within. You have to change your mindset. You have to change your language. You have to change your perspective on what is happening around you. If you say, "I am that house," "I am that car," I am that job," you will never lose it. How can you lose that which you are? Say with me, "I cannot lose that which I am." Your angel of prophecy is at work.

While Esau was engrossed in the business of hunting, Jacob lived within the life of his imagination. Let me give you a little secret. The secret to your success is to live within your imagination. Stop living within your paycheck. Live within your imagination! Stop living within your fear. Live within your imagination! Stop living within your job. Live within your imagination! Stop living within your lack. Live within your imagination! Your imagination is creation. Your angels are always working in your imagination.

The Bible says, *"As a man thinketh in his heart, so is he."* (Proverbs 23:7) Thoughts equate things. As we begin to imagine and think of things, those very thoughts will begin to manifest for us. It is very important that you have a healthy imagination in order to produce the right outcomes in life. God imagined us on earth and it was so. Imagination is creation. If you can imagine it, put an image to mind, it can come forth and it will manifest.

Principle #36

Live within your imagination.

Divine Deception

Rebecca never broke her prophetic connection. Her hope for Jacob was rooted in divine prophecy. There was nothing that could hold Jacob back. When God speaks a prophetic word over your life, He will bring the players into focus who are supposed be part of the fulfillment of that prophecy.

Rebecca's love for Jacob gave him the personality and the psychological strength that he would need later on in his life to begin to stand his ground. God began to set him apart, and Jacob manifested his prophetic word. He learned what he needed from within. He sought the supernatural, divine supply within him to manifest his prophetic destiny on the outside. Your supply is not going to come from the outside. Your supernatural supply is going to come from within.

Jacob's blind father brought him near him and said, "Come close that I might feel thee." Your angel set you up to feel like the blessing. You can only get what you feel like. Until you feel like it, it is unlawful for you to have it. Reverend Ike teaches that "feeling gets the blessing." Jacob's actions changed the entire birth order. He had to go out of his way to feel like the blessing. You will not get anything until you feel like that which you desire. You will not be prosperous until you feel prosperous. You will not be rich until you feel rich. You have to feel like you deserve it.

Sometimes our bodies do not know how to feel, so we have to tell it. But once we begin to decree and confirm the good, we begin to experience the good in our world. Feeling is always that aspect of you that is going to reap what you desire. That feeling is the energy reaching out into the ethers in the Spirit and pulling what you desire into your experience. You are not supposed to feel sick. You are not supposed to feel lack. You are only supposed to feel the good, because God is good. Until you feel like the blessing, it is unlawful to get the blessing. Your prosperity angel, your angel of increase, your retrieving angel are in your life from the day that the prophecy has been spoken into your life and dressing you up to feel like the part you are supposed to play.

Principle #37

Feeling gets the blessing. (Rev. Ike)

Feeling is the secret. The world and all that is within it is man's conditioned consciousness objectified. Rebecca was conditioning Jacob's consciousness so it could be objectified. You can think your way out of any situation in which you find yourself. Say with me, "I am thinking my way out of whatever negative situation I am in." Consciousness is the cause as well as the substance of the entire world. Nothing happens in the world without consciousness because consciousness is all that there is. It is to consciousness that we must turn if we are going to discover the secret of creation. You only get that which you are conscious of being.

There is no devil, no outside person that is trying to stop you from being, doing and having all that God has ordained for you. Jesus tells us that the devil is a liar since the beginning. (John 8:44) There was never a devil. The devil does not exist. You have the power to turn a lie into the truth in your own life. The only devil you will ever experience is the devil you create. The devil is a liar. This is the secret to living a victorious life. You only get in life that which you are conscious of being. The only thing that is blocking you is you. Jesus himself said, *"The prince of this world hath nothing in me."* (John 14:30) Jesus came to earth not to reveal himself, but to reveal yourself. Jesus came to earth to show you what you are supposed to be doing in the earth realm. Jesus chose 12 disciples, but he knew that one of them was the "devil." The only devil you get is the devil you pick, and when you are finished using that devil, or using that lie, then you cast it out.

Principle #28

The only devil you will ever experience

is the devil you create.

Jacob was a man that had to be conditioned before he could wrestle with an angel. Until you are psychologically fit and ready, it is unlawful for you to experience that which you are ordained to come into. Consciousness is the one and only reality. Once you understand the law of consciousness, you will create whatever you desire out of yourself. The conscious mind is the realm of effect. The subconscious, or as the psychologist Carl Jung would call it, the "collective unconscious" is the realm of cause.

There is a deep part of yourself that is causing everything that is happening outside of you. Therefore, you have to go within and trace that cause. What is in you that has caused you to stay stuck at your current salary? Somewhere you may have said in your former life, "If I can just make $60,000 a year, I will be happy." Now, your former life could be two years ago. You can only achieve the success that you are conscious of being. You have to cancel the former verbal contracts that do not line up with the truth of who God says you are. You have to override them. There are some things that I thought I would be happy with, and all of a sudden, I became miserable because they no longer met my needs. I became a different person. The person who receives the prophecy is a different person than the one who fulfills the prophecy.

I Will Be?

> *"Now faith is the substance of things hoped for, the evidence of things not seen." (Hebrews 11:1)*

The phrase, "I will be," is an enemy because it robs you of your present. When you say, "I will be," you delay whatever you desire. "I will be" means you are not that right now. The phrase, "I am," is in the present. It denotes manifestation right now. Faith is always now faith.

"I will be" echoes the sound of Lucifer who said, "I will be like the Most High." "I will be" puts you in a place that means that you are not there yet. "I will be" puts you at a future date. You have to begin to echo the voice of your mentor, not the voice of your tormentor. God's name is "I Am." Satan's name is "I will be."

The enemy will always try to put you in a state of "I WILL BE." The dying thief on the cross said to Jesus, "Remember me when you come into thy kingdom." But Jesus had to take him from the future to the present.

Jesus responded and said, "Today, you are with me in paradise." Never let the enemy put your blessing in an "I WILL BE" file. "I will be" will always put you in a false belief and false hope. It does not allow you to live in the now where things begin to take place, or allow you to come into your own true identity of I AM, which is everything.

Your angel works with your words. Your angels cannot work with "I WILL BE." Your angels can only work with "I AM." Sensation or feeling precedes manifestation. It is the foundation upon which all manifestation rests.

Many people have succumbed to a climate of fear because of what they are looking at with their natural eye. They see lack, limitation, a slow housing market, businesses closing. But their angel of prosperity comes to change their view and push them into a climate of faith—faith to do the impossible, faith to reach the unreachable, faith to do the unthinkable.

Many people are battling with two nations inside of them—one saying, "I AM healthy," the other saying, "I WILL BE healthy;" one saying "I AM rich," the other saying, "I WILL BE rich." You have to decide which nation you are going to feed. Rebecca knew in whom to put her stock and energy. She was grooming Jacob, while Esau was out in the field. Esau represents "I WILL BE," Jacob represents "I AM."

You may be reading this book and be among the millions of people who have lost their careers, their homes, their financial status. Can I tell you that God sends you to the prophet when you are in the midst of a crisis? Sometimes he sets up the conditions just so that you get in the face of the prophet.

Principle #39

Your angels can only work with "I AM."

5

The Angel of Feeling

"But let him ask in faith, nothing wavering, for he that wavereth is like a wave of the sea driven with the wind and tossed." (James 1:6)

The Cause of All Life

In the midst of this difficult period our country is facing, God's people are getting ready to experience quick breakthroughs and miracles in their lives. That is, if they are willing to apply the principles outlined in this book and work with their angels.

What you feel deeply is far more important than what you think. It is more important to feel it than to think it. When you feel something there is emotion, an energy and vibration, behind it. Feeling is so much stronger than thought. Before riches can manifest in your physical experience, you have to feel rich. It is not enough just to say or to think, "I am rich." If you do not have the energy and the emotion to go along with that thought, riches will never manifest in your experience.

If you don't feel a thing, it is not lawfully yours. You may think about doing something for a long time and never do it. However, when you feel something deeply, you are spurred into action and God moves. If a person does not act on their desires, it is because they have not felt those desires into their experience. They were just thinking about it. But when they feel it, they will start acting on it. Oftentimes, if someone is an heir to an inheritance, they feel entitled and are not motivated to feel it into experience. Sometimes when you are an heir you take it for granted, as if it is supposed to be given. The reality is that life only gives to the one who fights the good fight of faith.

Principle #40

If you don't feel a thing, it is not lawfully yours.

It is not how big the dog is, it is how big the fight is in the dog. Size does not matter. Have you ever seen a little dog force a big dog to retreat? Some people will not become rich because they never thought to fight for riches. They may say, for example, "If it's the Lord's will, I will be rich." Someone with this mentality does not have the fight in them. Not only is the Lord willing, he is able! But you have to be willing to fight. The Bible says to "fight the good fight of faith." (1 Timothy 6:12) We were never instructed to fight the devil.

Many people fight in the wrong direction. But what you fight you ignite. You feel the burn of that for which you are willing to step into battle. Keep in mind that God, the cause of all life, acts through the sense of feeling. God feels through you. So, He is touched by the feelings of your infirmities. He will fight with you when He can feel your need to act.

We must be doers of the word and not hearers only. If you only hear the word and refuse to take action according to all that is written therein, you deceive yourself. Until you do the word, it is unlawful for that word to become a part of your life and a part of your experience. If you are a hearer only and not a doer, you are like a man who observes his own natural face in the mirror and then walks away forgetting what he looks like.

Faith encompasses feeling. If you have faith, you will act. If you act, God-in-you is acting. Say with me, "God-in-me is acting through me." God continually acts through you, for God is your wonderful human imagination whose eternal name is "I Am." When Moses said, "Who shall I say sent me?" God revealed to Moses a name, "I AM that I AM." When we get the revelation of I AM that I AM, the eternal name of God begins to manifest in and through us. He acts only when you get to the point of feeling that revelation. If you don't feel it, God doesn't act on it. You have to make a decision whether you are going to believe the facts or believe the truth.

Co-Creators with God

Here is the truth of you. Say with me, "I am rich." You have to believe that you are rich. The facts may say that you are unemployed or your house is in foreclosure, but "I Am" who resides in you is rich. You just have to come into alignment with who God is in you. When you get into alignment with who God is in you, then God-in-you begins to demonstrate and walk the earth as you. You are too creative to experience recession.

The first recession is described in the book of Genesis, where there was no man to till the ground. There was a work stoppage. So, God said, "Let us make man." The way you stop a recession is by creating. You are a co-creator with God. God acts only when you feel it. God does not act until He can feel you act. You are the writer, the actor, the producer, the costume designer. God-in-you is producing Himself through Himself.

Principle #41

You are too creative to experience recession.

Nothing comes in your life without an invitation. Some people send out beautiful invitations for sickness. Others send out lovely invitations for recession to knock at their doors. Still others send out beautiful invitations for foreclosure. They send out invitations to their pity parties. Though they may not have asked for the situation consciously, their thoughts and feelings invited it into their experience subconsciously.

You do not attract what you want. You only attract what you believe to be true. Nobody receives that which they want because the only thing want produces is more want. Everything reproduces after its own kind.

You cannot have anything in life just by wanting it. You have to move from "I want that," to "I am that." Therefore, get into the spirit of mental conversations and give them the same degree of reality that you would a telephone conversation. You have to start mentally talking to your condition and start consciously living as if you already have it. Imagination is the beginning of the creation of all forms, and faith is the substance out of which they are formed. Nothing grows without imagination. Imagination is creation. Your prophetic angels point you to that which is great inside of you.

Principle #42

Nothing comes in your life
without an invitation.

Carry the Feeling

Poverty is consciousness. Prosperity is consciousness. Poverty and prosperity have nothing to do with how much money you have in the bank, the neighborhood in which you live, or the type of car you drive. You have the power to choose your level of living. When you give up your right to choose, you willfully imprison yourself. Things are not your reality. God is your one and only reality. You choose your reality by deciding what you want to be the consciousness of your being. If you want to be rich, then you must choose to infuse your mind with rich thoughts. If you want to live in poverty, then you will choose to infuse your mind with thoughts of poverty and lack. You have to train yourself to be poor because when God sent you into the earth realm, He sent you equipped with everything you need. You had to be trained to do without.

You have to carry the feeling of riches and prosperity in order to be prosperous. When you carry the feeling, you wear it. It becomes engulfed in you and you become engulfed in it, and you and the feeling become one. When you carry the feeling there is no separation between you and the feeling. Thus, manifestation is inevitable.

You have to embrace the assumption that you are the man or the woman you want to be. It does not matter if the outside denies it. It does not matter what the economy is saying. It does not matter how you look on the outside. You have to see the expressions on the faces of your friends and hear their congratulations on the inside of you. You have to have your celebration party on the inside. You have to experience the moving of God from within you. Your angels will visit you and show you the unfolding of God's blessings in your life from within.

Say with me, "I am carrying the feeling." The feeling is given to you for it to be carried. Reverend Ike says, "Life meets you the way you meet life." Life is waiting to meet you. It is all about your expectations and what you believe. If you believe that you are rich, if you believe that all is well, then so shall it be. If your expectation is that life is hard and things are going to be tough, then that is what you are going to experience. It is all about your expectation. According to your expectation, so shall be your manifestation. Everyone gets the manifestations of their own expectations. You have to begin to congratulate yourself on the inside with faith.

You have to clothe yourself with the feeling from head to toe. If you are not clothed properly, if you are not suited, it is impossible to have manifestation, because you are operating in a double-minded state of consciousness. You are cross-dressing. You have to be suited. When you are suited, everything matches—the hat matches, the bag matches, the outfit matches, the shoes match. Everything is suited. You have to be suited for manifestation. Say with me, "I am suited for the blessing." You also need the accessories because if you don't have the right accessories, you don't have "access." The outfit is incomplete. Life does not bless "Plain Jane." You have to go and fix it up in your mind. Now, this does not mean that you have to go out and buy designer clothes. I am talking about suiting yourself from the inside, where you visualize it in your imagination. You can only live what you imagine once you are able to walk in the manifestation thereof. You have to walk the red carpet in your mind before you realize the red carpet in life.

Principle #43

According to your expectation,
so shall be your manifestation.

Your feelings have to be steady. If you want prosperity, you have to feel prosperous. You have to think prosperous thoughts and you have to speak words of authority. You cannot say "I don't have…" "I can't do…" Your inner man has to be coordinated—your mind, your imagination, your thoughts, your feelings, the words you speak. Everything must be in sync. Whatever you believe will be externalized. What you feel inside is more important than what you think. Shakespeare said, "Assume a virtue if you have it not. A virtue must be felt to be assumed." You have to feel like money before you can assume a position that you are money. When you refrain from assumption one day, it will be easy to refrain the days ahead. When you refrain, you put another frame in your life. Some people have refrained from saying, "I am rich."

When you put on the coat of poverty you refrain from the good in life. It all begins in the mind. It is all about what you think. Until you assume the feeling from every fiber of your being, you are not going to experience it. The feeling has to be natural to you. It has to be in you. It cannot be forced or feigned. You have to naturally feel rich, naturally feel successful. The Bible says, *"Faith is the substance of things hoped for, the evidence of things not seen."* (Hebrews 1:11) Even though the evidence is telling you something else, you have to naturally feel the good; and because you feel it, you will become it.

You have to become one with the feeling. There cannot be any separation. The Mind and the body must be in agreement. You have to be it. If there is a separation, then your body and your Mind are not of one accord. You have to get to the point where the feeling overwhelms you and it tricks the Mind, because the Mind doesn't know the difference between imagination and reality. You can go from poor to rich in just one thought, as long as that thought is consistent. You can go from poor to rich with one sustained thought that, "I am rich." You cannot allow life to snatch it from you.

You have to eat that which you desire to be. You have to deceive yourself into believing that what you desire to be is real. You have to clothe yourself in the feeling of its fulfillment and then you will experience the feeling of satisfaction. You have to feast upon that which is good, so that your angel of faith can go to work and manifest it in your experience. Say with me, "I am ready to feast." Feast upon the feeling of "I am rich." Feast upon the feeling of "I am healed. I am accepted. I am blessed. I am loved." If you feast upon these feelings in the morning, in the noonday and at night, your desires will become a reality in your world because you are continually feasting on the right thoughts.

Principle #44

You have to feast upon that which is good, so that your angel of faith can go to work and manifest it in your experience.

Commanding the Hand of Your Angels

"Thus saith the LORD, the Holy One of Israel, and his Maker; Ask me of things to come concerning my sons, and concerning the work of my hands command ye me."
(Isaiah 45:11)

No one can demand to live according to their desires and that which they see in their mind's eye and then demand that someone else pay for their unhappy consequences. The Bible says, *"Man shall not live by bread alone, but by every word that proceeds out of the mouth of God."* (Matthew 4:4) When you operate according to the law of demand, you are the cause and not the effect. You are the creator of every situation you face in life. Therefore, you cannot be reactionary. You cannot react to the actions of others. Instead, you must operate as God, the creator of all things, and create the environment in which you choose to live.

You have the ability to command the hand of God. God has placed His angels around you so that you can command His hands. However, if you do not give your angels an assignment, you will never exercise your privilege to command the works of God's hands. You have the power to create the world in which you live. Whether you create a world of lack or a world of plenty, you create that world. You are the cause of your world. You act in mind according to your thoughts, and your material world reacts in direct response to your demand. You are the cause, not the effect.

Principle #45

You cannot react to the actions of others.

The demand you place on the universe reveals the service you will receive in your life. There is a presence in the universe that is personal to us. It is the spirit, of which we are the direct beneficiaries. Our individual ideas are a direct result of a demand that resides within us and which has been made upon the mind of God. Whatever we allow our mind to see, that is what we will be. Whatever we allow our mind to think, that is what we will experience in our world. Each person determines his/her level of living based on the limitations of their previous experiences. Whenever the universe makes a demand upon itself, out of that very demand is created its fulfillment.

$\mathcal{P}rinciple$ #46

You act in mind according to your thoughts,
and your world reacts in matter in direct
response to your demand.

Jesus said, "According to your faith be it done unto you." (Matthew 9:29) Everything that takes place in your life is based upon your faith. You cannot depend on your family, your friends, your parents or your job. You have to draw on the God-in-you and tap into the power to create the world that God ordained for you. Dependency is detrimental to your well being because it makes you look outside of yourself to another, when the answer is within you. Dependency will cause you to chase after the answer outside yourself instead of looking for the answer within. Dependency never allows you to grow and mature and come into your own, because you're always seeking the approval of others. When you operate in the spirit of dependency, you wait for other people to evaluate you and you fail to evaluate yourself. However, this behavior will stunt your growth. You will find yourself always depending on someone else to do what you already have the ability, capability and power to do for yourself. Dependency negates your oneness with God.

> *"Be ye therefore perfect even as your Father which is in Heaven is perfect." (Matthew 5:48)*

Man is commanded to be perfect. You are supposed to be Spirit free and not body bound. Many people have been bound in their body, bound by materialism, and seemingly have no control over their bodies. Instead, their bodies have control over them. This is not natural, this is not normal, and this is not the birthright of man. This condition has been imposed upon the human race that lives in ignorance of the principles that will make a people free. The Bible says, *"And you shall know the truth and the truth will make you free."* (John 8:32) You are only as free as the truth that you know. We need to understand how the false self operates. Life demands that you make decisions.

You have to repeat that which you desire over and over in consciousness until that reality becomes your experience. God throws us into dilemmas so that we can place a demand upon our angels. When demand is put into place then supply is of use. That is what faith is all about, doing that which is impossible. When the demand is made, supply will manifest and abundance is soon to follow.

Principle #47

Dependency is detrimental to your well being,
because it makes you look outside of yourself
to another, when the answer is within you.

6

The Angel of Faith

Now Faith

> *"NOW FAITH is the assurance (the confirmation, the title deed) of the things [we] hope for, being the proof of things [we] do not see and the conviction of their reality [faith perceiving as real fact what is not revealed to the senses]." (Hebrews 11:1) (Amplified Bible)*

Now faith is. Now faith is the presence, the substance, the ground support, the hupostasis (the basis or underlying foundation) of things hoped for, and it becomes the evidence of things not seen. Your faith is the title deed, the confirmation of all that you are destined to be, to do, and to have in this life. You do not need anyone to confirm that you are going to receive all that God has for you because your faith, your title deed, seals the deal. Your faith is the proof of things that you do not see with your natural eye.

Faith is an inside job. Faith is not something that you find outside of yourself. Faith comes from within. It is an all-knowing assurance that what God has spoken to you is true. Faith is consciousness. I am only as conscious as the faith I have. When I am conscious, I generate ideas that result in fulfillment and manifestation of that which I am conscious of being. Our consciousness is our faith. Since faith is the substance or ground support of the things for which you hope, then it must become your foundation. Your faith must become that upon which everything else stands. Until you produce faith for that which you desire, it is unlawful for it to exist in your life.

Principle #48

Your faith is the title deed, the confirmation
of all that you are destined to be, to do,
and to have in this life.

"For God, who commanded the light to shine out of darkness, hath shined in our hearts, to give the light of the knowledge of the glory of God in the face of Jesus Christ. But we have this treasure in earthen vessels, that the excellency of the power may be of God, and not of us." (2 Corinthians 4:6-7)

Faith is the priest that confirms the marriage of heaven and earth. Heaven cannot come into your reality until faith brings them together. "Have faith in God," actually means, have the God-kind of faith. We must have the same faith as God. Faith is the link between heaven and earth. Nothing leaves heaven until faith is produced on earth. "Yet we have this treasure in earthen vessels…" Heaven is waiting for your faith.

You cannot experience an effect without a cause. It is impossible to experience the effects of faith until you produce the cause, which is faith itself. Faith is the link. You have to produce the cause in order to have an effect. You have to keep faith in the forefront of your mind's eye (your consciousness). Faith is an act of consciousness, because consciousness is all there is. Faith is a state of thought.

"So then faith cometh by hearing, and hearing by the word of God. (Romans 10:17)

Principle #49

Faith is the priest that confirms the
marriage of heaven and earth.

Faith is reduced to a word. The component that makes you like God is your word because you have the ability to think. Not only do you have the ability to think, but you have the ability to form concepts and create worlds through your imagination. That is faith. No other creature on the planet is given the same ingredient as God, only man. Our ability to think and form our thoughts into things through our imagination requires faith in action.

Faith requires a knowledge that is certain. Faith is a knowing, a knowledge, founded on a firm belief. Faith is something that has to be consciously applied towards a definite purpose. What do you want to see God manifest in your life? You have to have something definitive in order for faith to operate on your behalf. You must be definite with the infinite. When you ask in faith you don't have to question whether it is going to be. It already is. Faith qualifies itself. *"For in him we live and move and have our being."* (Acts 17:28)

Do you think God performs miracles and then wonders if the miracles will manifest? Is that the God-kind of faith? That is not the way God operates. God operates from the place of knowing. You have to have the God-kind of faith, the kind of faith that allows you to rest in the fact that whatever you are believing God to do is already done.

We must learn to operate in the law of faith. Jesus said, "According to your faith be it done unto you." By this law man brings into his experience the things he desires. Notice, the scripture does not say, "according to your prayers," but according to your faith. God has nothing to do with the results that are in your life. It is all up to you. Your level of success goes in accordance with the power that you allow to work in you. The question is, is the power that is working in you faith or fear? If it is faith, you will see positive results. If it is fear, you will experience negative results.

Fear is faith in the negative. The Bible says, "God has not given us the spirit of fear, but of power, and of love and of a sound mind." (2 Timothy 1:7) God wants to move you beyond any situations that have negative consequences and move you into the realm of faith. We heal fear only by faith. Your fear can only be healed when you are operating in faith. Faith eliminates fear. F-E-A-R is an acronym for false evidence appearing real. Failure is evidence appearing real in your circumstances when you latch onto fear. Therefore, if fear is gripping your life and paralyzing you and not allowing you to move forward in whatever ventures you desire to pursue, you have to make a decision that you are going to do it, while being afraid.

Fear is an inversion of faith. It may sound strange, but it takes faith to operate in fear. You have to believe in fear to even experience fear, and then allow it to overtake your life. However, in order to overcome fear, you have to accept faith instead of fear. Faith overcomes fear. If you are not full of faith, you will be full of fear. You are either faithful or fearful.

Your angel of faith will usher you into the God-kind of faith and allow you to focus on the substance of the things for which you hope. When you operate in the God-kind of faith, you are able to eradicate fear and call those things which are not as though they were.

Principle #50

Fear is faith in the negative.

The Picture Frame of Faith

"Through faith we understand that the worlds were framed by the word of God, so that things which are seen were not made of things which do appear. (Hebrews 11:3)

The universe was formed at God's command. Yet what is seen was not made out of what was visible. That which you are going to create is not going to be made out of what is visible. Your freedom is not going manifest through what is seen. You are only going to demonstrate freedom by moving beyond your comfort zone. The characteristic that makes you like God is that you can form concepts and ideas. Say with me, "I love being like God." Animals cannot form concepts. The birds of the air, mammals, the fish of the sea, cannot form concepts. But man can form a concept. Man can form ideas.

Your angel of faith will cause you to will things into being. Your faith wills itself. Nothing comes into being until you will it. Our empowerment is a result of our ability to will what we desire into being. It is a power that can only come from within. When you turn within, your faith becomes quickened and you develop a renewed state of consciousness. You have to live in a renewed state of consciousness and make up your mind to be that state of consciousness, so that a renewed state of consciousness will start being in you. The moment a new state of consciousness begins to manifest in a person's mind, it is made evident by changes in his/her environment. Suddenly, they will start to love more; they will start creating wealth and prosperity in their experience; they will start broadening their inner circle and strengthening their network, because your network determines your net worth.

$\mathcal{P}$rinciple #51

Your angel of faith will cause you to will things into being.

"Now the LORD had said unto Abram, Get thee out of thy country, and from thy kindred, and from thy father's house, unto a land that I will shew thee: And I will make of thee a great nation, and I will bless thee, and make thy name great; and thou shalt be a blessing: And I will bless them that bless thee, and curse him that curseth thee: and in thee shall all families of the earth be blessed." (Genesis 12:1-3)

Abraham was a man of great faith. Whenever your angel of faith speaks it will always call you outside of your comfort zone. Abraham experienced this when he had to move to a strange land. His faith in moving outside of his comfort zone was rewarded in that wherever Abraham went things began to multiply. Abraham understood the power of faith and understood how to prosper even in a strange land. Your angel of faith will reveal to you the steps necessary for you to move towards manifestation of all that you desire.

Your faith will cause you to come into greatness. You have to get out of the place where you are and get to a new place that God will show you. God is in the business of showing you new places. Many people are frustrated in the place that they are because they are supposed to be on their way to a new place. God will frustrate your present to bring you to a new geographical location. He will cause you to become uncomfortable in your present economic state just so that you can experience prosperity. It is not God's will for you to remain in the same state that you are in today. God's desire is that you go from glory to glory, from a great level to an even greater level.

"I will bless them that bless thee and curse him that curses thee. And in thee shall all families of the earth be blessed." (Genesis 12:3)

Principle #52

Your angel of faith will give you witty
inventions that will bring abundance
and prosperity into your experience.

God wants to make you a great nation. God wants to make your name great. God took Abraham, a stranger, and promised to make his name great. Not only that, God promised that Abraham shall be a blessing to others. Your angel of faith will give you witty inventions that will bring abundance and prosperity into your experience. You have to develop a product or a system where you and all families of the earth will be blessed. When you bless others, God blesses you.

Therefore, you must go within and develop the right concepts so that you can bring abundance and prosperity into your present and sustain it in your future. The "I" is the part of you that forms the concepts, gets the ideas through the law of being and the law of faith, and then forms the ideas that begin to move you into the renewed state of consciousness. There is a dream inside of you that is larger than you and is ready to be expressed in the universe. There is a dream that will bless you greatly and richly benefit the families of the world. However, you must first develop your "I". You cannot develop ideas when you hate yourself. Ideas and money only come to people who love themselves.

It is hard to become wealthy and have self-hate. The Bible says, "Love your neighbor as yourself." The only way you can bless others is if you love yourself. When you love yourself, you will be able to develop correct concepts, ideas and ideologies that will allow you to dream dreams that will bless the world. It is important that you begin to look at the quality of your life. People cannot love you more than they love themselves. If a person abuses drugs and/or alcohol, they do not love themselves. If they do not love themselves, how can they love you? If they choose to destroy their own body, then it is safe to say that they are incapable of loving you. Toxic relationships affect your "I Am" consciousness.

Principle #53

Toxic relationships affect your "I Am" consciousness.

Faith-Filled Ideas

Faith in the unseen God brings you into divine guidance. God promises that he will guide us with his eyes. You must have faith in the unseen God. If you cannot have faith in the unseen God, then it is unlawful for the unseen God to have faith in you. Consciousness is always calling you to seek out a new country, a new state of being, a new place of awareness. Consciousness is always calling you into another realm.

Until you become conscious of expansion, expansion will not be conscious that you exist. Life is just waiting for you to lift up your eyes. The moment you start lifting up your eyes, things will start rising for you. Jesus lifted up his eyes to heaven and the bread started multiplying. Everything in life waits for you to give it a lift. You have to lift up your eyes above material things and see only Spirit. All things are ready when the mind is ready. When you still your mind, you will begin to see the manifestation of your desires. You must fix your eyes on the future until your future becomes fixed in the present moment.

Abraham always worked in the realm of now faith. Now faith is clearly filled with substance. Everything is waiting to be filled with substance. Your faith goes forth to bring into manifestation that which you need. Faith becomes the very substance of things hoped for, and then it becomes the evidence of things that are not seen.

Principle #54

Substance cannot appear until your faith becomes real.

You only have as much money as you have faith in your ability to obtain money. Faith is the substance. If you desire to have substantial money, you have to have faith that you can attain it. You have to believe it. Substance cannot appear until your faith becomes real. When your faith is present, then your substance is seen. We must bring the faith of God into the multitude of manifested thoughts and actions. It is not enough to plan. You must have action to bring that which you believe God for into being. Faith brings God into manifestation through your very thoughts and your acts. God comes into being only to the degree that you are able to have faith and believe. The universe is waiting to support you, but it needs something substantial with which to work. The size of your dream will reveal the greatness of your God. The size of your dream will reveal the inner workings of your consciousness. How big is your dream?

It is the awakening of the human consciousness that will bring us into the fulfillment of our dreams, hopes and desires. All that God has for you is just waiting for you to wake up. When you wake up, things will start moving for you. However, it is not enough just to wake up; you have to take action. You have to put your feet to the floor. Faith only works when we add motion to our faith. The Bible says, "Faith without works is dead." You have to put feet to your prayer. You have to put feet to your faith. You have to put feet to your thoughts. Everything requires corresponding action.

Faith produces ideas. Faith will allow you to have an internal knowledge that if you can think it, it will happen. Reverend Ike says, "If you can think it up, you can think it down." Your angel of faith will cause you to develop ideas that will manifest and come to full fruition. Your faith is like a seed, and the ideas come harvesting after it is sowed. The power of faith produces your thoughts and ideas. Without faith nothing would be possible, for we know the worlds were framed by faith. Don't be conscious of poverty, lack, depression, sickness or disease. Be conscious of health, wealth, prosperity, happiness and joy. You will experience that which you are conscious of being. Your faith has to connect with your will for you to experience manifestation. Your faith wills your desires, hopes and dreams into being.

Principle #55

Faith produces ideas.

Your faith must be deliberate. You have to hold the picture of that which you desire in your mind's eye and then bring the body of that idea into manifestation. You have to hold on to the thought and not allow anything to deter you from the manifestation thereof. You have to live a life worthy of that which you desire. You have to hold it in your consciousness and know that you deserve it. As you begin to hold on to it, it shall come to pass. You can't quit. You can't doubt. You just have to believe, knowing that what you desire is the truth of your being. When you start operating in the truth of who you are, those things are going to come into being.

Principle #56

You will experience wealth as a result of your faith-filled ideas.

You will experience wealth as a result of your faith-filled ideas. When you start producing faith-filled ideas, you will experience bountiful supply. Your faith is really creating the ideas which will bring forth supply. You will always express your most dominant idea in body consciousness. I am fulfilling my dominant ideas right now in my present body. If you do not like the dominant ideas that are presently in your experience, then you must produce a stronger idea. You will always express your most dominant ideas in body consciousness. How ready are you to embody the next level of consciousness for your life?

Substantial Faith

Whatever we hope for mentally, we must begin to see it with our mind's eye and see all the possibilities that are connected with it. Nothing becomes substantial until you see it mentally, with possibilities. Faith resides in the unseen realm. Our faith results in the manifestation of our thoughts, our dreams, our hopes and our desires. Everything starts in the realm of faith where you mentally see it, mentally conceive it, mentally achieve it, and it manifests as thoughts and acts.

> *"As it is written, I have made thee a father of many nations, before him whom he believed, [even] God, who quickeneth the dead, and calleth those things which be not as though they were. Who against hope believed in hope..." (Romans 4:17-18)*

The God-kind of faith calls those things which are not as though they were. But even when hope is against you, believe in the very thing that is against you and know that it is going to turn for you and work out in your favor. What scene has life painted before your very eyes which appears to be against you?

> *"Who against hope believed in hope, that he might become the father of many nations, according to that which was spoken, So shall thy seed be. And being not weak in faith, he considered not his own body now dead, when he was about an hundred years old, neither yet the deadness of Sarah's womb. He staggered not at the promise of God through unbelief..." (Romans 4:18-20)*

Principle #57

Our faith results in the manifestation
of our thoughts, our dreams, our hopes
and our desires.

Abraham did not even consider that he and Sarah could conceive a child. Here is a master key. When the picture of life is painted against you, do not be weak in faith by **considering** your own circumstances. The moment you consider your circumstances, you diminish your faith. You have to hope against hope so that you can become. Do not consider the facts! Don't consider your bills. Do not consider your circumstances. To consider such things constitutes weak faith.

How do you stagger at a promise of God? Abraham did not stagger at the promises of God, but was strong in faith. When you stagger at the promise of God you enter into a realm called "unbelief." Not only was he strong in faith, but right in the midst he gave glory to God. Faith puts you into a realm where you do not operate according to common sense. When you operate according to your common sense, you fail to walk in miraculous faith. There is no unbelief. There is no distrust that would make you waver. For Abraham, there were no doubting questions, nothing in his mind that would cause him to doubt or to negate the promise of God, because he believed.

Principle #58

Don't consider your circumstances, for
to consider such is weak faith.

7

Destroying the Gatekeepers

As A Man Thinketh

"For as he thinketh in his heart so is he." (Proverbs 23:7)

What is a gatekeeper? Proverbs 23:7 says, *"For as he thinketh in his heart so is he."* The Hebrew word for "think" is *sha'ar,* which means, "to act as a gatekeeper." According to the etymology dictionary, the word "think" means, "to exercise the mind; to judge; to consider; to propose." The mind is the place where thinking occurs. It is the place where you take in new ideas and relate them to some of your existing ideas or destroy certain ideas and mindsets.

Oftentimes, people are defeated because of the various cycles that they go through in their mind. Low self-esteem, poverty, lack, fear and depression, just to name a few, are cycles that destroy the mind and stop our productivity. People who suffer from low self-esteem not only make themselves miserable, but they make everyone around them miserable. Individuals who suffer from low self-esteem find it very difficult to love their neighbor. The Bible says that you must love your neighbor as yourself. If you do not love yourself, you cannot love your neighbor. Oftentimes, people treat others negatively because they have a negative self-image. They put down others to make themselves look good.

You may be suffering from low self-esteem and praying for deliverance from the demon of low self-esteem. No! You don't need deliverance. You don't need a devil cast out of you. You need to change your thinking. You need to change your mindset. You need to renew your mind.

Principle #59

Low self-esteem, poverty, lack, fear and
depression, are cycles that destroy
the Mind and stagnate our productivity.

Still there are others who suffer from extreme frustration because of the lack that exists in their lives. Why are some people not prosperous? It's simple—80 percent of working people are doing jobs that they do not enjoy doing. Money is not the issue. Poverty is a mindset. Lack is a mindset.

*"But his delight is in the law of the LORD; and in his
law doth he meditate day and night." (Psalms 1:2)*

Another definition for "think," according to Webster's Dictionary is, "to turn something over in the mind; to determine; to reflect." Research has proven that it takes six repetitions of an idea before the new information becomes a part of a person's consciousness. Think about it—a thought must be repeated at least six times before it is converted into a mindset. The only way to combat negative thoughts and negative mindsets is to do what the Bible suggests, meditate day and night. Instead of letting the television "watch you" while you sleep, and wake up at 2:30 or 3:00 in the morning from disturbing dreams (people coming out of the grave, and bones standing in front of you) go to sleep listening to peaceful, meditative music, or watching television programs that will help you think positive thoughts and meditate on the awesomeness of God. You need to learn how to fill your atmosphere with the word of God.

Principle 60

The only way to combat negative thoughts and
negative mindsets is to meditate day and night.

Some people watch television all day. As soon as they come home from work they turn on the television. Television is one of the most damaging past-times in our society. People feel that if they keep their children off of the street, keep them out of the hands of the drug dealers and prostitution, then they would escape a lifestyle that will be the cause of their demise. However, many of the programs on television bring those very lifestyles into the home. I often refer to the television as the "one-eyed demon." Has the "one-eyed demon" been watching you lately? What has it been programming in you while you have been asleep?

You must also be cognizant of the music that you listen to and allow your children to listen to. What messages are being conveyed through it? We need to guard the ears of our young people. You cannot walk in the things of God and walk in the world at the same time because you will find conflict. There is a conflict of interests. It's not going to work.

The most miserable individual in the world is a backslider. Once you walk in the fullness of your "I Am" state of consciousness and taste of the heavenly gifting of God, it is impossible to operate according to the world's mindset. No matter how hard you try to fit in, you just won't fit. The backslider doesn't fit in the world and he doesn't fit in the church. If they go into the church, the odor of the world is on them. If they go into the world, the odor of the church is on them.

Some of you have been there. You try to go back into the world and do your own thing, and all of a sudden conviction sets in. All of a sudden you start hearing your pastor's voice. You're in the middle of doing your own thing, and all of a sudden a prophecy comes back to mind that was given to you two years ago. You leave off the dance floor and you feel empty. You think to yourself, "I don't have it like I used to have it." The reason is that God has put his hand on you.

You have to learn how to destroy the gatekeeper. You have to destroy negative thoughts and ideologies. You have to get rid of stinking thinking. According to the *Theological Wordbook of the Old Testament,* the word "think" comes from the root word which means "gate; to split open or to break through." Your thoughts are your gatekeepers.

The Bible says that you are a city that is set on a hill. (Matthew 5:14) Every city has gates to it that allow entry and exit. Who is sitting at the gates of your city? What mindsets do you have that refute the word of God in your life or that are contrary to the gospel of Christ? What thoughts are screening the events of your life? Some of the gatekeepers that are sitting at your gate are robbing you of your prosperity. Some of the gatekeepers that are sitting at your gate are robbing you of divine health. Some of the gatekeepers that are sitting at your gate are robbing you of the abundant life.

Principle 61

The wrong gatekeeper will allow negativity to overrule your life and smother your dreams.

How are they robbing you? They are not allowing truth to enter into your consciousness. When opportunities for wealth are presented to you, your gatekeepers say, "No, that cannot happen for me." "That is too good to be true." "I guess I am going to be poor for the rest life." Many people are taught that the government is "big brother." So, people are conditioned to always have their hand out looking for something to be given to them. Then they go to church with the same mindset, always looking for a handout.

In order to be successful in life and enjoy the abundant life that God promised, you must get rid of the poverty mentality. You must cast down the gatekeepers of lack, limitation, and scarcity. The wrong gatekeeper will allow negativity to overrule your life and smother your dreams.

What gatekeepers are sitting at your gate? What are you allowing in your city?

Renew Your Mind

Depending on the size of the city, the city had a varying number of gates, but there was always one main gate which consisted of an outer and an inner gate. In other words, although there was one main gate, people who entered discovered that there were other entrances into the city. When you don't have the word of God, when you don't have Jesus sitting at the main gate of your city, anything and everything has access into your "city." Paul said, *"Be not conformed to this world, but be ye transformed by the renewing of your mind."* (Romans 12:2) Your guardians sit at the gate of your city, standing watch and waiting to destroy the negative gatekeepers that try to infiltrate your mind.

The city was extremely important in the life of the people because there, at the gates of the city, was where the social, administrative and business transactions occurred. People would go to the gate of the city to find out the news of the day. If you wanted to know the latest news in the city, you went to the gates of the city.

Your mind has to be renewed because God wants to put up the proper gatekeepers, the thoughts that will bring abundance to your life, the thoughts that will bring peace, wholeness and divine health to your life. You need to block the entrance to the negativity and the rubbish that could be waiting at the gates.

Do you want to know what the members of your body are doing? They are rushing to the gate of your city to find out what new piece of news is coming up. If the prophet tells you that healing and divine health are coming your way, but your gatekeepers say, "No, it's God's will for you to be sick," you need to renew your mind and destroy those negative gatekeepers. You have to constantly and consistently check the gatekeepers of your mind to ensure they are operating in accordance to the will and plan that God ordained for your life.

The thieves of doubt, insecurity, lack, poverty, sickness, disease and fear, just to name a few, can destroy your mind. They are improper gate-keepers. But there has to be a "being" before a "becoming." Your mind must receive the thought before it can be made flesh. The transformation begins within you.

Fear vs. Faith

"Wherefore I put thee in remembrance that thou stir up the gift of God, which is in thee by the putting on of my hands. For God hath not given us the spirit of fear; but of power, and of love, and of a sound mind." (2 Timothy 1:6-7)

People experience defeat and misfortune in their lives because of the thoughts that are sitting at their gate (the opening of their mind). There are certain fears that are hereditary. There are some cycles of defeat that have been passed down from your parents. These thoughts can be classified as mindsets. But there are only two fears that are natural, the fear of noise and the fear of falling. A child will immediately respond to both. All other fears are learned.

The gifting and talents within you must be guarded and guided. After they are guided, then they have to be given unto others. A gift is not something for you to keep personally. God gives a gift for it to be passed on. God did not deposit the gift of the prophet within me for my own personal gratification. The gift of the prophet was placed in me from the foundation of the world to bless others. However, that gift had to be guarded from birth. If you fail to guard the gifts that God has given you, the enemy will come in and prostitute them and then they never become the vessels or gifts of honor. Instead, they become gifts of dishonor.

If fear resides in your temple you must destroy that gatekeeper. God has not given you the spirit of fear. The thief, your adversary, your negative gatekeepers have allowed that thought to penetrate your being. In Greek, "fear" means, "timid or cowardice." God does not give you a spirit of timidity. The righteous are bold as a lion. If you are afraid of witnessing, there might be something wrong with your righteousness. Anything that is not worth dying for is not worth living for. You might as well pack your bags and get out of here.

God does not want his people to be cowards. God cannot use cowardly soldiers. God said to Timothy, "Stir up the gift that is in you." Timothy let the spirit of fear keep the gift of God from coming forth in the fullness that God intended. Many people fail to meet their full potential in God because of fear. Fear will paralyze your faith.

According to *Webster's Dictionary,* "fear" is, "the instinctive emotion aroused by impending or seeming danger, pain, or evil; terror; sudden peril; panic." Animals operate by a fear instinct, survival of the fittest. When you move in fear, your emotions begin to take control instead of your Spirit being led through hearing from God. Your animal instinct begins to override your "I Am" nature and you operate outside of your true nature.

Fear stunts your potential. It will stop you from achieving greatness in your life. Fear will stagnate your success and cause you to miss your divine destiny. You can change your destiny by destroying the gatekeepers that are in your mind.

> *"And we know and believe the love that God have to us. God is love, and he that dwelleth in love dwelleth in God and God in him. Herein is our love made perfect." I am going to show you how your love is made perfect that we may have boldness in the day of judgment: because as he is, so are we in this world." (1 John 4:16-17)*

As God is, so are we in this world system. God called us to this world system to become a standard to the kingdom of darkness, that when light appears, it makes a clear statement that darkness must disappear. 1 John 4:18 says, *"There is no fear in love, but perfect love casteth out fear because fear has torment. He that feareth is not made perfect in love."* If you operate in fear, that means there is an imperfection in your love. The opposite of love is not hate, but fear. When perfect love comes on the scene it casts out all fear.

Seven Keys to Eradicating Fear

1. Pinpoint how you acquired the fear.

Sit down and begin to take a review of your life. Go deep within the recesses of your mind, as early in your childhood as you can remember. As you go through the events of your life, write down the incidents that occurred in your life that caused the spirit of fear to emerge. After you have written down every incident that you can remember, begin to destroy the negative thoughts that are connected to the event.

2. Destroy feelings of fear by applying the word of the Lord.

Some of the fear that you have is hereditary, passed down through three and four generations. Why aren't you successful in business? You may have been programmed for years to go out and get a good job, especially a government job. So, when the Holy Spirit says, "I want you to go in business for yourself," the gatekeeper says, "No, you want that good government job." Mindsets. Fearful thoughts can come through your parents and family members or they can come through friends and acquaintances. If you associate with people who are not doing anything with their lives, then chances are you will do nothing. If you associate with people who have no drive or ambition, then chances are you will not have drive and ambition. If you associate with people who are not going anywhere, chances are you will not go anywhere. If you hang around with people that are unemployed and don't have any money coming in, before long you will find out that you are unemployed. You need to fly with the eagles, and get away from the buzzards.

3. Destroy the fear of lack.

Fear of lack comes from a poverty mentality. Certain myths come with the fear of lack or the fear of poverty, such as, "hard work produces wealth." The people who work the hardest get the least. Now, I am not suggesting that you do not work. You need to work. But you also need to learn how to use your mind. A lot of manual work will not make you rich. If you don't believe it, think about the factory workers. They get a half hour lunch and two 15 minute breaks, and are making minimum wage. That is a myth.

Another myth is, "It is not right for you to enjoy yourself and get paid." In other words, work is work. Many people believe that they are not to enjoy their work. But that is a myth. You should like what you are doing. If you don't like what you are doing, then you are in the wrong profession. The people that become successful are those who enjoy what they are doing. When you only do what you are told, then you are a slave. When you do more than what you are told, you are free.

4. Destroy the mindset that there is not enough to go around.

God created this earth. Do you think that God does not know how to run His planet? Do you think that He would cause the earth to populate and there not be enough resources in the earth to accommodate everyone? We have already proven that money is not the answer to poverty. We have enough money to wipe out poverty. But there will always be poverty because there are those who have a poverty mentality. Poverty is not dollars and cents. The poorest man is not a man without a cent; it is the man without a dream. Do you have a dream?

5. Destroy the fear of aging.

The fear of aging holds many people back and stunts their growth. It is said that your mind does not reach its peak until it reaches 70 to 80 years of age. Those who have become forgetful before 70 and 80 have been short-changed. We only use about eight percent of our mind in a lifetime. Einstein used 10 percent and was considered a genius. Think about it. Destroy the fear of aging and allow God to elevate you from glory to glory.

6. Destroy the fear of criticism and rejection.

People who become successful in life are shakers and movers. Successful people do not worry about what others think of them. Successful people are not constantly looking for approval and affirmation from others. Successful people are confident with who they are in God and are determined to operate in their "I Am" nature. You are not out to make people accept you. Just make them respect you. Do you think everybody accepted Dr. Martin Luther King, Jr.? Do you think he sat around and worried, "I wonder if they are going to accept me? Do you think they will accept my message?" He would have never made it. The individuals that become something for God are shakers and movers.

7. Destroy the fear of success.

Ignorance and fear are like a pair of shoes, they are always together. Success requires a greater level of thinking, a greater level of awareness and a greater level of mastery. However, many people fear success because they unconsciously do not want the increased responsibility that success brings. If you are open to the increased level of responsibility and commitment and allow yourself to believe that God will bring your provision for the vision, then you can destroy the fear of success and move into the greatness that God has ordained for your life.

8

The Angel of Prosperity

"Beloved, I wish above all things that thou mightest prosper and be in health, even as thy soul prospereth."
(3 John 1:2)

Christ Consciousness

God is in you. The Bible says, *"Greater is he that is in you than he that is in the world."* (1 John 4:4) So, why are you looking for a God outside of you? The fool hath said in his heart, there is no God (Psalm 14:1). The "fool" is the person who does not see God within and chooses to connect with God outside of himself. The one who holds the key to your destiny, the one who holds your prosperity in the palm of His hand, the one on whom you should lean is your divine self, the God-in-you. The God-in-you is all life and encompasses all that you need to be successful in this life.

Get excited about the fact that God is in you. There are no poor people, only people who are not aware of the riches of God within. The poor are those who are ignorant of the rich resource provided by the presence of God in them.

Your subconscious mind accepts whatever ideas you feed it and brings those ideas into your experience. You must have the attitude that you are a winner. Live with the understanding that health is wealth. You must sleep with the feeling that you have the power to overcome any obstacle. God's gift to you is your ability to shape your life as you want it to be. Have you thanked God for the gift he has given you? Life treats you the way you treat life. All good things are possible when you look to the presence and power of God within.

Whatever you hope for, whatever you pray for, all of your dreams can be found in Christ. And He lives inside you. Christ in you is the hope. What are you hoping for? It can be found in the Christ that is in you. Until you recognize that you are the Christ, you have no hope. When you just refuse to be Christ, when you refuse to stand in Christ's stead, then you are operating in the spirit of the anti-Christ.

Principle 62

Life treats you the way you treat life.

Do not deny yourself the privilege of dwelling in the I Am consciousness, because life meets you like you meet life. There is no will of God outside of you to impose itself on you. If you want prosperity to manifest in your life, you must operate in the I Am consciousness. Money only comes to those who proclaim, "I am money." Whatever you have in consciousness you will have in your experience.

Soul Prosperity

Do you believe in yourself? Believe in yourself first and others will believe in you. Prosperity and health walk hand-in-hand. Your soul prosperity determines the success of your relationships. Soul prosperity determines the return you will receive for your actions. The soul is the seed of your emotions. The soul is the place where you think, the place from whence you exercise your faith. Therefore, if your soul is prosperous, your exercise of faith will yield greater return.

Two things the Apostle John wished for you, health and wealth. You have to make those wishes come true. Philippians 2:5-7, says, *"Let this mind be in you which was also in Christ Jesus. Who being in the form of God thought it not robbery to be equal with God. But made himself of no reputation, and took upon him..."* He went from form to form, from glory to glory—prophetic shape shifter. How do you remove the obstacles in your life? You have to change forms. How do you move the mountains in your life? You have to change forms. You have to go to the mountain and watch it transfigure.

Many people have been changing shapes all of their lives, but have not been aware of the transformations. The problem is they have allowed other people to shape them instead of taking the initiative to shape themselves. When you allow others to shape you, and you lack the power to shape yourself, you are under the influence of witchcraft.

It would be similar to someone saying, "Since you don't know what you want to be, I'll just make you a cow."

God created man in His image. Notice, he did not form man in His image. Although we are from the same Creator, we all form differently depending on our individual thoughts, opinion, ideologies, relationships, dreams and beliefs. Don't lose sight of the fact that it is all about imagination, because imagination is creation. God is our imagination. Those who do not realize that God is their imagination never truly find God. True prosperity is when you can finance your imagination. That which is a possibility is no good to us until we make it a reality.

Principle 63

Although we are from the same Creator,
we all form differently based on our
individual thoughts, opinion, ideologies,
relationships, dreams and beliefs.

When God creates, He has all of the puzzle pieces ready before He starts giving it form. Infinite money, divine intelligence, all of the promises of God are already in front of you, but you have to open your eyes and begin to see what God sees. Some people are too lazy to see the picture that God created for them since the beginning of time. For some reason, they think the harvest was easy to manifest. The Bible says that the Lord of the harvest would send forth laborers, which means that you are not going to experience the harvest without labor. The farmer has to go out in the heat of the day to harvest his crop. In the same way, you have to bend and put yourself in uncomfortable positions and conditions so that you can reap the fruit of God's promises in your life. Reaping the harvest requires work.

You are the creator of all things. So, you formed the devil that is on your trail with your imagination. The ignorance that plays itself out in your life, you formed it. Matthew 6:33 says, *"Seek ye first the kingdom of God and his righteousness, and all of these things shall be added."* If there is no understanding of the concept of the kingdom of God, then things will not be added. Things are only added to kingdom seekers. The kingdom has to be your priority. You have to seek the God in you. You have to seek the power of God that is resident within you. Then, you will experience soul prosperity.

You determine your level of prosperity. You determine everything that you will be in life. Everything comes to you in a state. All consciousness is a state of being. You are in a state of being right now. You can change states in a moment. You can change states in the twinkling of an eye. The Bible says, we shall be changed, in a moment, in the twinkling of an eye. (1 Corinthians 15:52) This is a reference to the twinkling of our third eye, the eye of our imagination, the eye that is the real window of our spirit, the eye that is the creator of all things. If you change your third-eye vision, then your sate of thought changes as well. If you can change your state of thought, then thought will manifest as reality and usher you into a new state of being. That's creation!

Principle 64

If you can change your state of thought,
then thought will manifest as reality
and usher you into a new state of being.

You are a co-creator with God. You create darkness. You form the light. You create the madness and then you give it order. When you have had enough of playing the fool, you say to the universe that you are ready to enter into a new state of being, a new state of consciousness, the place of prosperity. To go from poverty to prosperity you are going to go through various states. You're going to go through the state of discipline. You're going to go through the state of money management. You are going to go through the state of relationships. You are going to go through the state of networking. Every one of those states will help you get to the state in which you want to live. Every state is a point of revelation, a new awareness. You can go from poverty to prosperity in a moment. All you have to do is put poverty asleep and become aware that you are rich in substance.

Purpose + Thought = Manifestation

> *"The Lord of Host have sworn saying, surely as I have thought so shall it come to pass and as I have purposed so shall it stand." (Isaiah 14:24)*

Your thoughts bring things to pass. Anything that you want manifested in your life, you have to think and purpose it. Notice, the scripture does not say you have to say it, because the Bible understands that thought is already a declaration in itself. *"For as a man (or a mind) thinketh in his heart, so is he."* (Proverbs 23:7) Thought does not happen in your head, but thought happens in your heart. Your thoughts are the language of your heart and your imagination. You are speaking at all times in your heart.

Every thought is a prayer. Every thought I have, whether good, bad or indifferent, will come into my experience. Now, you may be saying to yourself, "I think about money and prosperity all the time. Why haven't I experienced them in the natural?" What other thoughts do you think about during the day that may crowd the thoughts of money and prosperity? The only way to get the treasure out of your mind and into your life is by thinking right thoughts into being. You have to get the filth out of your mind because it is blocking the treasure from coming forth. Every excuse is a blockage. An excuse is nothing more than a guarded lie. When you give an excuse you just block your blessing. You are giving the justification of why it cannot be in your life. Every excuse undermines faith, and focuses on the material. True faith is your ability to look beyond the material and see the reality.

Nothing can happen to you unless it happens through you. You have the power to bless yourself. You have the power to prosper yourself. Your prosperity does not come as a result of something outside of you. Your prosperity comes from within. As long as you believe your prosperity is something that comes from outside of you, you will experience hell in your life. Nothing can happen to you, whether good, bad or indifferent, unless it happens through you. You cannot have a car accident unless you already had one mentally. All sickness begins in the mind. The body has never been sick. The only thing that has ever been sick is the mind. The cancer patient goes to the surgeon to remove the tumor and in a few months it grows back again. Why? The source of the pain was not treated. The source of the pain was the mind.

Principle 65

Thought does not happen in your head, but thought happens in your heart.

Paul said we must be transformed by the renewing of our mind. If you want to be financially transformed, you have to renew your mind. Notice it doesn't say, "Be ye transformed by the **removal** of your mind." Removal does not bring transformation. Renewal brings transformation. Total well-being must happen in and through you in order to happen to you. I cannot experience total well-being unless it is already happening through me, emanating from within. Good health must happen in and through you in order to happen to you. In other words, you must have healthy thoughts, a healthy appearance, and behold healthy images. Happiness must happen in and through you before happiness can happen to you.

Love must happen in and through you before love can come to you. If you want friends, you must show yourself friendly. In order for people to love you, you have to first love yourself. Until I love myself it is impossible to love anyone else, because people who are hurting can only hurt people. Success must happen in and through you in order to happen to you. The question is, how do you picture yourself? How do you envision yourself in this hour? How do you project yourself?

One of the things I discovered later in my Christian walk was that I was operating in faith, but I had my faith in people. I was telling God who to work through to bless me, instead of placing a demand on the God-in-me to bless me. My faith was in the wrong place. My faith was in man, instead of in God. My faith was in that which was outside of me, instead of the God within me. There have been times when my children come to me and ask me for something and I tell them no because I see that they put their faith in me instead of in God. Is your faith in the right place?

Principle 66

Nothing can happen to you unless it happens through you.

Prosperity must happen in and through you in order to happen to you. I see myself prosperous. The economy is not my reality. I look at the economy for entertainment purposes only. Never look at the news unless you have the ability to see beyond the material and see the reality. When Jesus went to the tomb of Lazarus, he did what Paul said in Thessalonians—*"shunned the very appearance of evil."* Jesus did not see death in the tomb; he saw resurrection. Every divine mind must lift its sights, its inner vision, to see beyond materiality and envision reality.

Every millionaire, before they became millionaires, had to think like a millionaire. Every billionaire, before they became billionaires, had to think like a billionaire. When you start having millionaire thoughts, you will see the millionaire status manifest in your experience. Millionaires will start to come into your circle. You meet no one but you. Fish swim in schools; horses run in herds; birds fly in flocks; winners associate with winners; and losers associate with losers. Who you walk with reveals who you are. You attract your likeness, not that which is foreign to your nature. If you want to measure your growth in God, look at the environment that you magnetize.

You may be wrestling with materiality at this very moment. Your checkbook may not balance. You may have a rich man's dream with a poor man's pocketbook. But the way to remedy this situation is not by getting a second job. You will just be poor at a higher level. The way you get out of the mess you are in is by giving yourself a mind cleaning. Your mind is like a merchantman, always buying and selling. Buy the success idea instead of the poverty idea. Buy the idea that His yoke is easy and not the idea that there are hard days coming. What is your mind buying?

Money must happen in and through you before it can happen to you. You have to become money; you have to feel like money; you have to confess with your mouth, "I Am money." Until you can feel it, you will not see fulfillment. You have to get full of the feeling. Even a mother has to feel the baby kick and have labor pains before she can feel the baby in the crib. Nothing in this universe gets translated into being without emotion. Your prosperity angels will bring purpose and thought together and create the manifestation of prosperity in your experience. You just have to put your prosperity angels on assignment and command them to go out on your behalf and show you where your riches lie.

$\mathcal{P}rinciple$ 67

Your prosperity angels will bring purpose and thought together and create the manifestation of prosperity in your experience.

Let Go and Let God!

> *"And God said, Let there be lights in the firmament of the heaven to divide the day from the night; and let them be for signs, and for seasons, and for days, and years: And let them be for lights in the firmament of the heaven to give light upon the earth: and it was so. And God made two great lights; the greater light to rule the day, and the lesser light to rule the night: he made the stars also." (Genesis 1:14-16)*

Contrary to popular belief, God does His best work in the dark. He starts in the evening and works all through the night. He never sleeps nor slumbers. God said, "I formed the light. I created darkness." God divided the day and the night; the "light" from the "darkness" within himself. We talk about the devil being the enemy of God, but actually the Scripture says the carnal mind is the enmity of God. This is the first great separation of thought—consciousness. The division of light and darkness demands a distinction and separation of the mind of the flesh and the mind of God.

God is the beginning, the cause, the source of all that is. Therefore, stop holding on to the past because the past is not worth holding on to. Learn to accept the gift that God has given you. You have the ability to make your life what you want it to be. Affirm in your Spirit, "It is no longer I, but it is Christ." Know that you are a prophetic shape shifter. You can shift today. If you are overweight, you can be underweight. If you are underweight, you can be overweight. If you are poor, you can be rich. If you are sick, you can walk in divine health. All you have to do is put your mind to it. If you need attention, don't create an emergency. Do something else more creative. You choose your state of mind. When God brought every animal to Adam to see what he would name them, He was giving Adam the power to name his environment. Look at the wisdom of God. He wanted to see what Adam would name them. That is the gift that God has given you. You have the ability to name your surroundings and your circumstances. He is looking at you to see what you are going to call the situations and circumstances that are happening in your life. Give them a prosperous and positive name, and your state of mind, and as a consequence, your experience in the natural, will change.

Repeat after me, *"Thank you, God-in-me, for this beautiful imagination, which is creation. You've given me this gift of life. Thank you for the revelation of God and the ability to perceive my purpose. Thank you for the grace to become all that I am ordained to be."*

The will of God is your ability to will your destiny into being. What good are you if you can't manifest destiny? Become the co-creator. If you only knew the power that is within you, you would never be powerless again. It is the God-in-you who is working all the miracles outside of you and around you. Allow your angel of prosperity to work within you and push you into your manifested destiny!

Principle 68

God is the beginning, the cause,

the source of all that is.

9

The Art of Working with Your Angels

"Behold, I send an Angel before thee, to keep thee in the way, and to bring thee into the place which I have prepared." (Exodus 23:20)

Personal Magnetism

"Beware of him, and obey his voice, provoke him not; for he will not pardon your transgressions: for my name is in him." (Exodus 23:21)

There is an art and a science to working with your angels. Your angels have been sent before you to prepare the way for you. Your angels are working on your behalf. There is a certain magnetism, a connection, that takes place between you and your angels. However, you have to be careful how you work with your angels so that you don't provoke or grieve them. Your angels are here to work for you, and assigned to work overtime on your behalf. They are working on your behalf to keep your enemies at bay.

> *"But if thou shalt indeed obey his voice, and do all that*
> *I speak; then I will be an enemy unto thine enemies, and*
> *an adversary unto thine adversaries." (Exodus 23:22)*

There is a strong personal magnetism between you and your angels, a divine connection that works for your good. Your angels will be enemies to your enemies, and adversaries to your adversaries. Your angels are in your personal atmosphere. They absorb and respond to whatever affects you. Your personal atmosphere is controlled by the content of your consciousness. Your angels work with that which you are conscious of being. Jesus always said, "According to your faith be it done unto you." What you hold in your consciousness is what your angels will assist in manifesting into your experience.

Principle 69

Your angels work with that which
you are conscious of being.

God has equipped you with a personal magnetism that enables you to attract whatever thought you hold in consciousness, whether good, bad or indifferent. God has equipped you with a perseverance and determination to develop your magnetic ability and cause you to pull the good into your orbit. However, you must be determined and willing to persevere in developing a God-consciousness that will attract the good that God has ordained for your life. Then, your angels are dispatched on your behalf to help manifest it in your experience.

> "I beseech you therefore, brethren, by the mercies of God, that ye present your bodies a living sacrifice, holy, acceptable unto God, which is your reasonable service. And be not conformed to this world: but be ye transformed by the renewing of your mind, that ye may prove what is that good, and acceptable, and perfect, will of God." (Romans 12:1-2)

God has equipped us with two distinct abilities, mental ability and physical ability. Making this distinction and understanding how your thoughts manifest in your experience is key to your success, happiness and prosperity. Nothing moves unless the mind moves it. Thought first takes place in the mental body and then manifests itself in the physical body. Therefore, the correct movement of thought is vital. Your angel is looking at you continually to see what you are moving with your mind. That is his cue to take action.

Holy living is also very important. There is a part of us that has to feel worthy of the very thing that we desire. There are many people who never come into their prosperity because they have never felt worthy of it. Holiness does not bring you to salvation, but it somehow gives you the internal license to say, "I am due." Say with me, "I am due for a breakthrough."

Principle 70

Your angel is looking at you continually to see what it is that you are moving with your mind.

Therefore, you cannot be conformed to this world or thoughts and beliefs of the world. You have to have thoughts that transcend the world's thinking and move into the realm of the Divine Mind. According to Reverend Ike, "You are either casting a spell or the world is casting its spell and you are catching it." Simply put, you are either casting or catching. Reverend Ike referred to the "gospel" as the "God-spell." Which spell are you casting? It has to be the God-spell. The God-spell or the gospel is the good-spell, which is the healing spell, the prosperity spell, the blessing spell, the angel spell. The angels are sent into your life to minister the things concerning the gospel.

If you fail to understand the God-spell, you will miss the good that God has for you and you will find yourself struggling and living according to the world's spell. You have to be careful not conform to this world, because as you conform to the world, you become the world to which you conform.

Principle 71

Understanding the process through which your thoughts manifest in your experience is key to your success, happiness and prosperity in life.

Conscious Projection

> *"And thine ears shall hear a word behind thee, saying, This is the way, walk ye in it, when ye turn to the right hand, and when ye turn to the left." (Isaiah 30:21)*

Interaction with your angels involves two important components, the mental and the physical (the mind inside of you and the physical body that is carrying out what is happening in the mental world). When you understand the mental world, you will start to understand the spiritual world. There is thought transference going on between you and your angels. Your mind projects, and forces outward mental vibrations that create an atmosphere in which you can minister and do your spiritual work.

The physical component produces generational blessings that are based on generational thinking. God works in generations. However, He works in generations according to your thoughts. Every individual has a physical magnetism. Lawyers interact with lawyers; orators interact with orators; physicians interact with physicians; ministers interact with ministers. When you understand that you are a great mind, you will gravitate to other great minds. For example, when your consciousness begins to evolve to a greater level, the books and materials that you need to educate and elevate your mind will begin to surface because the mind is ready to receive them. You would not be able even to read this book unless you were ready to start working with your angels.

Principle 72

God works in generations.

Your angels are reading your consciousness. According to Theron Q. Dumont in his book, *The Art of Personal Magnetism,* "Your mental state of who you are creates the mental atmosphere and charges the vibration so that there can be a conscious projection of the mental currents from the brain's center by the actions of the will of the individual." Everyone has vibration from their mental center, the atmosphere that is created in your mind (your heaven), which creates the situations and conditions that you experience on a day-to-day basis. Angels pick-up on these vibrations and use them to define what your mental center has accepted as your atmosphere.

Your angels are always working with your consciousness because consciousness is all there is. As you become aware of what God is doing within you, you will experience breakthrough around you. God is getting you ready for a fruitful season. Not only do you have an angel who goes before you, but you have a word behind you, pushing you forward. Once your angel clears the way before you, he works behind you, pushing you forward in the direction you need to go. You need to hear what the word behind you is instructing. The question is, can you do what the word behind you is commanding you to do?

Your angels are always reading your Spirit and your thoughts. They create an aura around you and ensure that the right people are around you according to your personal vibration. The Spirit of man is the candle of the Lord; it illuminates His moving. (Proverbs 20:27) Hebrews 1:13-14 says, *"But to which of the angels said he at any time, Sit on my right hand, until I make thine enemies thy footstool? Are they not all ministering spirits, sent forth to minister for them who shall be heirs of salvation?"* Your angels are ministering spirits. Because you are an heir of salvation, your angels are assigned to minister to you. The words spoken by your angels are sure, and come as a result of what your spirit and thoughts are telling them of your needs and desires.

Principle 73

Once your angels clear the way before you,
they are behind you pushing you forward
in the way you need to go.

"Therefore we ought to give the more earnest heed to the things which we have heard, lest at any time we should let them slip. For if the word spoken by angels was stedfast, and every transgression and disobedience received a just recompence of reward; How shall we escape, if we neglect so great salvation; which at the first began to be spoken by the Lord, and was confirmed unto us by them that heard him." (Hebrews 2:1-3)

You are projecting something right now. Say with me, "I am projecting prosperity." Everyone has mental forces. Everyone operates within the will. Paul said, "It is no longer I that liveth, but it is Christ." Christ is the will of God in men. *"Christ in you, the hope of glory."* (Colossians 1:27) When you start projecting the will of God within you, you will start bringing forth your divinity. Your angel is aiding the release of your divine self. Your angel is aiding you in getting ready for your prison break. Some people have been so trapped in body consciousness that they never know how to be spirit-free. However, there is a conscious projection that emanates from the renewed mind. You have a personal atmosphere that is at work. Your angels give color to your atmosphere. The degree of color depends on your level consciousness regarding what you are feeling, and the level at which you are vibrating. Therefore, it is vital that you renew your mind from within. Your vibration must reflect consciousness of who you really are.

The Picturing Power of God

"Therefore I say unto you, What things soever ye desire, when ye pray, believe that ye receive them, and ye shall have them." (Mark 11:24)

Your angels work on your behalf according to your desires. Everything that happens in your life starts with a desire. Here is another master key. When you pray, believe that you have received and you shall have. Why would Jesus tell you to believe that you receive it? The object of your prayer is not to get something from God. It is to give yourself permission to have something. It is to own the object of your desire. This is the power of assumption. Your angels love when you assume an identity. The moment you assume a new identity, your angels go to work to deliver it to you.

You are the imagination of God at work. The word "imagination" really has no definite meaning. The dictionary defines "imagination" as "the picturing power or the act of the mind; constructive or creative principle." Your imagination is the picturing power of God in action. Therefore, when you pray, imagine that you have already received the object of your desire and imagination will make sure that you have it.

Principle 74

You are the imagination of God at work.

Imagination is the gateway of reality because your mind's eye imagines it. Can you unload all other thoughts in your mind and retain only that imagined thought? Assumption will only happen if you are loyal to that image. The reason why some people do not see the manifestation of their desires is because they have an external "lover." You say, "I am rich," but you are flirting with poverty. You say, "I am wealthy," but you are flirting with a budget." If you are completely loyal to that which Spirit desires to give you and enter into imagination, you will begin to see some things happening in your experience that will turn your life around.

Christ is your imagination. Therefore, your imagination is your redeemer. Whatever it is you need to be redeemed from, all you have to do is imagine it. Whatever you want to be freed from, all you have to do is imagine it, and your imagination can rework your situation.

Man becomes what he imagines. Your angel is engrossed in your imagination. Say with me, "I become what I imagine." You are becoming what you are imagining at this very moment in space and you are creating it in time. Facts are the fruit bearing witness to the use or the misuse of your imagination. If you are experiencing lack in your life in any form, it is simply the misuse of your imagination. If you are experiencing sickness in your life in any form, it is simply the misuse of your imagination. Man only becomes what he or she imagines. Instead of you "taking it to the Lord in prayer," you must go within and raise that thought to another level because God has already declared that "it is finished." You only become what you imagine.

Principle 75

Man becomes what he/she imagines.

Imagination is the way, the truth, and the life revealed. Everyone lives in the revelation of their imagination. Neville, one of the great mystics, says, "Natural man sees a bud, imagination sees a full budded rose." Natural man sees a seed, imagination sees a harvest. Natural man sees lack, imagination sees the harvest that is abundant and overflowing.

God is not mocked. Whatsoever a man sows, that is what he/she shall also reap. (Galatians 6:7) Those who are spiritual, do not mock or deny the outer world. We understand that it is the continuous working of the inner world within ourselves (imagination) that keeps redistributing our outer world. The day I live in today will not be the same day I am going to walk into tomorrow. My tomorrow is determined by today's workings of my inner self.

Angel Work

Your angels are working in your imagination, firmly planted in it, ready to move forward into demonstration. Imagination and faith are the secret of creation. "Without faith it is impossible to please God." Why is it impossible to please God without faith? Where there is no faith, there is no creation. God loves himself, so he loves other creators. You are a co-creator with your Heavenly Father.

Your angels are working in your active imagination. Your consciousness is the light reflected in the mirror of your mind and projected in space to the one about whom you think. Every time you are thinking thoughts about others, you are projecting those thoughts into space and into consciousness. This is how you work with the angels of other individuals. When you need something done, you talk to the angel of that situation.

In the book of Revelation, John says in his salutation, "To the angel of the church of..." John spoke to the angels of the different churches. There is a being over your situation and you have to learn, through your imagination, to speak to it subjectively. This is angel work. I speak to the angels of my children. I speak to the angels of those who have authority over me and who will see me in the light of the favor of God. I speak to the angels of those who owe me money and I say, "Repayment angel, let them pay swiftly and quickly. I see good coming unto them."

Principle 76

Your angels work in your active imagination.

You may have tenants occupying your property who are late in making their payments. Instead of fighting with them and expending that valuable energy, go into your mental body and work subjectively with their angels. Have your angel take their angel to court and do it on the level where principalities judge quickly and swiftly. Their angel will begin to be that voice behind them saying, "This is the way, walk ye in it." Speak subjectively to the angels and they will begin working on your behalf.

"And, behold, a woman, which was diseased with an issue of blood twelve years, came behind him, and

touched the hem of his garment: For she said within her-
self, If I may but touch his garment, I shall be whole. But
Jesus turned him about, and when he saw her, he said,
Daughter, be of good comfort; thy faith hath made thee
whole. And the woman was made whole from that hour."
(Matthew 9:20-22)

The woman with the issue of blood said within herself, "If I can touch the hem of his garment, I will be made whole." She did not touch a physical garment, but she touched one of the ethereal bodies of Christ. That is why Jesus was able to recognize that someone touched him. He did not say, "Someone touched my garment;" he said, "Someone touched me," because he felt virtue leave him. The power was not in the garment, but it was in the Spirit of Christ, something far greater than the garment. She was touching Spirit. She moved beyond that which was physical and began to move into the Spirit realm.

The woman was able to work with her mental body. According to St. Matthew, the woman said within herself what she needed to do to invoke her healing. Mark 5:30 says, "Jesus immediately knowing within himself…" Notice how they were both speaking with each other subjectively. There was no exchange of words. There was no outward conversation. There was only inner conversation. This is the art and science of working with your angels.

This was an inside job. Here is another master key. To change the world you must first change your concept of it. Many people will not see change until they change their perception. You have to learn how to fall forward and stop falling backwards, for that which you are conscious of being is your reality. Consciousness is the one and only reality.

Principle 77

Consciousness is the one and only reality.

10

The Power of Angel Writing

The Divine Secret of Asking

"And I say unto you, Ask, and it shall be given you; seek, and ye shall find; knock, and it shall be opened unto you. For every one that asketh receiveth; and he that seeketh findeth; and to him that knocketh it shall be opened." (Luke 11:9-10)

As we have read throughout this book, angels are special agents who carry out the divine assignments of God. Effective communication with your angels is paramount to your success in life. There is power in writing to your angels. Writing to your angels is sacred because when you write to your angels you invoke them to respond to your desires. When writing to your angel, you are writing to your higher consciousness. Bringing that higher consciousness to yourself will allow you to evolve into a state of complete awareness.

Writing solidifies your desires. When you write to your angels, your desires are five times more likely to manifest. Writing allows you to bring all the members of your being together into one consciousness and bring that which you desire from the realm of the Spirit into the realm of manifestation. You can write to your personal angels, the angel of your enemy, the angel of a friend, or the angel of a situation or circumstance. When you write, you make the assignment you want your angels to carry out clear and definite.

You may think that angels should already know what you want. So, why bother them by asking. This thinking might come from an inner struggle of past actions or thoughts. You may have been in a relationship where you thought the other person should have been able to read your mind and/or know your thoughts. The only possible result to this expectation is the disappointment you experience when the other person does not read your mind. This misunderstanding has ruined many marriages, friendships and business relationships. In order to get what you want in life you must take a positive step and set into action the divine secret of asking.

Principle 78

When you write to your angels you invoke
them to respond to your desires.

There is no harm in seeking your angels for guidance because they only operate in favor of the highest good. By writing your dreams, goals and aspirations on paper you are at the beginning stages of working with your angels.

The Process of Angel Writing

"And there were in the same country shepherds abiding in the field, keeping watch over their flock by night. And, lo, the angel of the Lord came upon them, and the glory of the Lord shone round about them: and they were sore afraid. And the angel said unto them, Fear not: for, behold, I bring you good tidings of great joy, which shall be to all people." (Luke 2:8-10)

Write the following declaration 10 times…

"ANGELS OF PROSPERITY, COME TO ME RIGHT NOW!"

The written word is said to have a special power of its own. Declaring your wishes on paper and addressing your letter to the angels is a good way of clarifying your goals and desires. To make a special request to the angels, take a piece of paper and address it to your personal highest angel and the highest angels of the others your request involves. In your request, be specific and define what you desire as clearly as you can. Always add the phrase, "for the highest good of all concerned" to your note. Then express your gratitude. Thank the angels as if the request has already been granted. Also, thank God and all of those who have something to do with the request. As you exercise your faith and write to your angels, you will begin to see your situations change right before your eyes. As you begin to write the vision and make it plain, you will gain clarity in the power of writing to your angels.

Writing is the first step toward manifestation. When we write, we pull what we desire to manifest from the Spirit into the earth realm for people to see and experience. Writing is a very powerful tool that God has given us. As we visualize what we desire and write it down, we hasten its manifestation. When we write, we increase the speed of manifestation five times. Writing hastens the process and solidifies your desire in the earth realm.

Principle 79

Writing is the first step toward manifestation.

The following are the steps to implement when writing to your angels…

1. Purchase a special notebook that you will use exclusively for writing to your angel. The notebook should be considered sacred and should only contain your requests, petitions and declarations to your angels.

2. Develop a strong sense of faith and belief that what you write to your angels is going to come to pass. If you do not believe it will come to pass, don't write it.

3. Declare that your request, petition or declaration has already manifested even before you see the physical manifestation in your experience. Remember, you have to feel the blessing before you can experience the blessing. You have to feel like money, before money can manifest in your world.

Some people have not communicated with their angels since they left heaven. It is important to keep our connection to the angels that God ordains to walk with us in life. Angels understand the language of writing. When you write to your angels, you employ them and invoke their services on your behalf. You begin to send your angels on assignment to retrieve that which has already been ordained for you by God. Your angels are waiting for you to employ them and send them out on assignment on your behalf. However, when you ignore your angels or fail to send them out on assignment, you put them in a holding pattern and essentially, delay your blessings.

If you ignore someone, he/she will eventually leave your presence. The same is true of your angels. When you do not communicate with your angels, they will stand idly by and take no action on your behalf. Where your energy goes, that is where the power will flow. By writing to your angels you acknowledge them and transmit energy to them. This will cause them to begin to work on your behalf. Rather than neglecting them and leaving them unemployed, you're giving them energy and recognition and allowing them to move on your behalf. As you write to your angels, that which you desire will start to instantly manifest.

Principle 80

When you write to your angels, you employ them and invoke their services on your behalf.

Writing to your angels is particularly effective during the New Moon, a time of new beginnings. Writing to your angels during this time allows you to set your purpose and intent for what you want to happen in the next season of your life. In scripture, when the woman's son died, she made a decision to go see the prophet to find out the answer to her dilemma. Her husband's response was, "Why are you going to see the prophet, it is neither new moon nor Sabbath." The woman knew that the New Moon heralds the dawn of a new season. Whether you write to your angels during the New Moon or on the Sabbath, or at any other time, is not really the most important element. Your angles are forever in worship, so the specific time is not the essence. What truly matters is that you make a determination to write to your angels so that you can put your angels on assignment and experience manifestation in your life. Writing to your angels positions you for a turnaround in your life.

> *"For we do not wrestle against flesh and blood, but*
> *against principalities, against powers, against the rulers*
> *of the darkness of this age, against spiritual hosts of*
> *wickedness in the heavenly places." (Ephesians 6:12)*

Not only can you write to your angels, but you can write to someone else's angels—a friend, an enemy, a family member, spouse, co-worker or associate. Oftentimes, when people encounter a problem with another individual, they attempt to deal with the individual one-on-one. But the Bible says we wrestle not with flesh and blood. It's not flesh and blood that we should contend with, but it is powers, and principalities and spiritual wickedness in high places. So, when you write and address the principality or address the angelic being that is guarding that individual, their angel will tap the person on the shoulder and say, "Be kind to Johnny because he had the unction to talk to me and you did not." Write to the angels of people who are causing you problems.

> *"Unto the angel of the church of Ephesus write; 'These things saith he that holdeth the seven stars in his right hand, who walketh in the midst of the seven golden candlesticks.'" (Revelation 2:1)*

The scripture clearly says, "Unto the angel of the church of Ephesus write," which means you can write to the angel of an institution. Write to the angel of your creditor before you go to do business. Write to the angel of the situation before you start dealing with the situation, because there is a principality, a principle that can only be dealt with in the Spirit, overseeing the situation. There is an angel guarding and taking charge over your specific situation.

Writing to your angels positions you
for a turnaround in your life.

Paul wrote to the angel of the church of Ephesus, "These things said he that holdeth the seven stars in his right hand..." The right hand denotes the hand of honor, glory and power. The seven stars represent the seven planetary systems. God was holding Hermes, also known as Mercury. He was holding Aphrodite, also known as Venus. He was holding Aries, also known as Mars. He was holding Zeus, also known as Jupiter. He was holding Chronos, which you would know as Saturn. He was holding Apollo (the Sun). He was holding the Moon. He was holding the seven stars, which is how we get the seven days of the week, starting with Sunday, which is the Sun's day; Monday, which is the Moon's day; Tuesday, which is Mars' day; Wednesday, which is Mercury's day; Thursday, which is Jupiter's day; Friday, which is Venus' day; Saturday, which is Saturn's day.

Could it be that the seven stars are always picking up what we say? That is why the science of interpreting the stars is called "astro-logy," meaning, the speech of the stars, or the words of the stars. Astronomy means "astros" or stars, and "nomy" in the Greek is "law," which is the law of the stars. There is the law of the stars, which is definitive and sci-entific, which denotes where the stars are situated in the universe. Then, there is the speech or the discourse of the stars, where the stars are speaking to one another. Your angels are waiting for your words to be expressed among the stars.

Letter Writing to Your Angels

Writing a letter to your guardian angel is a very effective way to make contact. You should begin to keep a journal to help you write letters to your angels. The time, thought and effort you put into writing a letter to your angels concentrate your energies and focus your spirit. You will be surprised how you will make contact with your angels while in the process of writing the letter.

Your guardian angel is always around you. Although angels are always around you, waiting to do your bidding, many people don't see their guardian angel until death. Many people still have their angels unemployed. They are going to be amazed when they transition from this life and realize that they lived a life of struggle or poverty because they never employed their angels to help them. They never asked their angel to assist them. Your angels are at work. Your angels are willing and ready to help you.

There is no need to write in a formal manner when writing to your angels. Write your letter to your angels like you are writing a close friend. Obviously, have a purpose for writing your angels. If you have not yet made contact with your angels, you might write asking for a closer connection so that you can start to get your angels working for you. Tell your angels about your family, your relationships, your work, your plans, and your dreams. You talk with your friends, family and associates. Why not talk to your angels? You will find this practice to be far more beneficial.

Writing down your hopes and dreams forces you to give them definition and clarity in your mind. This will effectively start to turn them into goals that you can pursue as you start writing to your angels. If you are worried, you need to write to your angels so that you can employ your worry angel. Your angels are here to work for you.

Principle 82

The time, thought and effort you put into writing a letter to your angels concentrate your energies and focus your spirit.

Appendix

Define Yourself!

Define and declare who you are.

"And in the morning, as they passed by, they saw the fig tree dried up from the roots. And Peter calling to remembrance said unto him, 'Master, behold, the fig tree which thou cursedst has withered away.' And Jesus answering saith unto them, Have faith in God. For verily I say unto you, that whosoever shall say unto this mountain, Be thou removed, and be thou cast into the sea, and shall not doubt in his heart, but shall believe that those things which he saith shall come to pass; he shall have whatsoever he saith. Therefore I say unto you, what things soever ye desire when you pray, believe that ye receive [them], and ye shall have [them]." (Mk. 11:20-24)

The scripture says, "Have faith in God." Have the God-kind of faith. It also means have the same faith that God has. A mountain is nothing but a vibration. You have to learn how to talk down every vibration that tries to be an obstacle in your life. All thoughts are things. So you have to say to the mountain, "Be thou removed!"

What do you desire? What is it you want in life? What are you believing God for in life? *"What things soever you desire..."* The crowd will try to kill your desire. There is something around you right now that is killing your desire, killing the very feeling of prosperity in you. There is something growing around you that does not belong to you. It is like a weed, a seed that has gone bad.

The scripture says, "what things soever ye desire when you pray, believe that ye receive [them], and ye shall have [them]." What do you have to do? BELIEVE! What do you have to believe? **You have to believe that you have already received that which you desire.** Until you believe that you have ALREADY received, you will not have!

Weak people will make you weak.

Weak people say they cannot attain their goals. But do not lower your standards. If you are not careful, weak people will have you thinking weak. You will start thinking the way they think, and then you will start doing business the way they do business. You have to remove some people from your life right now.

Define what you want to be.

Do you know what you want to be? You have to define yourself. When you know what you want to be, declare who you see yourself as being.

Define what you want to do.

What do you want to do in life? You have to define what you want to do, and then make sure that nothing pulls you away from what you are called to do. You have to watch for the distractions. A distraction will send you out of orbit, out into space, to a place where you are not supposed to be. A distraction will turn you into a weed.

Define what you want to have.

Do you know what you want to have? Until you know what you want to have, you will not have it. Define what you truly desire. Define whether you are in the right place to obtain it. However, one of the things you have to understand is that the right place can become the wrong place when the lease is up. God told the Prophet in 1 Kings 17:3-4, *"Get by the Brook Cherith, for I have arranged for the raven to feed thee there."* But, once he got there and stayed for a while and got comfortable, the brook dried up. Why did the brook dry up? Because his lease was up, his time for being at that specific place had expired. You must know when your lease is up; when that particular season has ended.

All relationships are not lifetime relationships. Some relationships are seasonal. Some relationships are for seasons, and some relationships are for reasons. You have to discern who you are with at each specific moment. Are you with a person for a season or a reason, or are you joined together for a lifetime? You have to be clear on whether a relationship is for a season, for a reason, or for a lifetime. Otherwise, you will try to hold onto a season for a lifetime. If you don't watch the season you are in, you might try to carry a season over into another season in which it is not meant to continue. Perhaps God has given you someone to walk with you for a reason and now the reason has been fulfilled. Are you trying to make the reason a continual season?

When you understand your seasons you will not be misplaced. When you understand the reason for being at a place, you will not be displaced. However, when you are not in place, you will be frustrated. Why? Maybe you don't understand your season. People say, "I want to do my passion." It's good to do your passion if you are disciplined. If you are not disciplined, you should stay away from your passion because your passion will be spoiled. I hear a lot of people say they want to do their passion, but they are not yet ready for the responsibility doing their passion entails.

You should stay away from your passion until you are disciplined because your mind may not be ready to handle the success the passion can bring. If that is the case, you will be derailed instead of you staying on track.

Some people are good at what they do; however, their lifestyle is so shabby that it takes away from the beauty of what they can do. Never deliver a person out of a place because they may be there for a reason. They may be in that place to become disciplined so they do not move out of season. They have a great gift, they have great passion, but there is no discipline in their life, and when there is no discipline, there is no standard.

If you have no standard, you will corrupt your gift. A gift that is not guided is destructive. Therefore, define what you want to have.

> ## You must come to a point of self-definition.

Everything in life is bringing you to a point of self-definition. Every day I ask myself questions before I retire. If I have a free moment during my day, I may walk down to the lake, and sometimes I ask myself the question, "Am I profitable today?" And then I wait and answer myself. Thinking is hard work. Thinking will ask you some tough questions.

Sometimes I ask myself the question, "Do you deserve to remain on the planet today? Have you been profitable to society?" If you keep telling yourself the wrong thing long enough, you will eventually begin to believe your own lie.

> ## You must have positive self-awareness.

Are you positive about yourself? Ask yourself, "Am I being productive in society? Am I increasing those that I am with? The person to whom I am assigned, am I making them great?" The Bible says that until you make another man great, God will not give you that which is your own.

When a great man calls you to do something, that is a gift. It means that God is testing you to see if you are ready to receive your own. If you are not faithful in that which belongs to another man, then God will not give you that which is your own. Simply put, you did not pass the rites of passage test. Go back to kindergarten. You have to start all over again because the wrong response to a situation you were given during a rite of passage could become the wrong decision you make on the battlefield in the midst of war. It could become the cause for the loss of all the spoils or even the entire platoon.

When we talk about taking the land, owning real estate, taking over property, putting up developments, building houses, let me tell you something, that is war! There will be individuals who will say, "We can't let you have this. We are not going to give that up easily because we brought you here in this community to be working hands. We brought you in this community to be renters. We brought you in this community to be "down and outers" not "up and outers." We brought you into this community to be beggars. We brought you into this community to work in our hotels. We brought you into this community to be little workers, walking around in the streets with hopelessness in your face. We brought you into this community to wash our floors. This is what you are here for." But when you start to change the picture, it is war!

When you start telling people to lift their heads up, when you start telling people to look like they know where they are going and walk like they know where they are going, when you start lifting the sights of people, then people cannot stay in their downtrodden state. It is a war zone!

Psalms 37:37 says, *"Mark the perfect [man], and behold the upright: for the end of [that] man [is] peace."*

"Mark the perfect man." When you find a mature person, imitate him/her. If you are working with someone, look like them. Mark them. Look at the way they walk; look at the way they talk; look at how they carry out their duties. Mark the mature man. Mark the perfect man. Then, follow his/her lead.

> **"My Divine self is what I am in God and what God is in me."**
> **(Rev. Ike)**

Living bread is the positive concept of good. When you partake of living bread you are getting a hold of a positive concept of good. If you stop feeding the manifestation (concept of yourself) that you do not like, it will die out of your experience.

Put your negativity on a diet. If you put it on an extreme diet, it has to die. Kill it! Stop feeding any manifestation which is a concept of yourself that you do not like.

You are feeding whatever is in your experience. You are chopping down the wood and putting it in the furnace. Stop feeding any manifestation that is not the truth of you! When you stop feeding it, it will stop living in you. You have to starve it out of your experience.

> **Do not give the God-power of your attention unto negative, unworthy ideas and concepts.**

Don't give the God-power (thought power) of your attention unto negative, unworthy ideas and concepts. If you stop thinking about certain people, they will also leave your existence. If you are not careful, people will ground you and you will find that you can't get off the ground because now you are in a babysitting service. There are spouses who cannot leave their home today because their mate is on a drug of some type. They say, "Now, let me hurry up and get back home." Why? They are concerned their spouse might sell everything in the house.

However, they could starve that person out of their existence by not feeding it. Change the locks. What is it that you're keeping alive that should be dead?

Man is the manifestation of his own self-concept.

You are a manifestation of your own self-concept. So, create a positive, and prosperous, concept of who you are.

Man is a manifestation of his inner consciousness (beliefs, ideas and self-concept).

Be careful who you allow around your children. Children are like clean pieces of paper. Everything that touches them leaves a mark. Children absorb information through feeling. You cannot put your children in just any daycare. Even when they become teenagers, you have to watch who they play with. Who they interact with might become their new parent (guiding figure).

The Bible says, "Train up a child." When you look at a train you see tracks. Children have to be kept on track. A wrong relationship will derail your child. You have to make sure the people who influence your children hold the same ideas that you hold for them.

A grandparent can take your children off track if they don't hold the same values that you hold. For example, you may say to your son, "Listen, you need to stand up and really be a man." The grandmother may say, "Oh, no, they're just a baby. Come over here and let me hold you." They're taking them off track. If they see two heads in a house, they are seeing duality. They are seeing a split nature. If you don't govern your household, your children will get off track.

> **Manifestation does not exist (live) of itself (alone).
> The source and sustenance of all manifestation is inner
> consciousness (the mouth of God.)**

The sustenance of all things is the inner consciousness, the mouth of God. Consciousness is the objective and the vivid manifestation. All manifestation desires to be seen.

Any manifestation, whether it's good or bad, stays sustained by the inner consciousness. That is the only way it exists. It is only maintained because of the consciousness you have within. You have to ask yourself, "What are you feeding?" Negative people can't stay around you unless negativity is in you. Negativity is fed by the inner consciousness, and will live as long as the inner consciousness of it exists.

You have to destroy the inner consciousness that is feeding it. Every so often you have to have a kingdom checkup and affirm, **"The kingdom of God is within me!"**

Affirmation

Thank you, God-in-me, for the truth of God which resonates in me. I decree and declare that the Presence of God in me creates new realities around me and through me. I decree that the Presence of God in me awakens me to a new state of consciousness, a new place of being. I decree that the Presence of God-in-me creates fabulous new realities in everything I say and do. I thank you, God-in-me, for being God-in-me. I thank you for the truth of God, which is me. God-in-me, be my supply. God-in-me, be my source. God-in-me, be my reality.

I decree and declare that my angels are working overtime on my behalf to bring the good that God has for me into my life. Prosperity angel, go to work and open the doors that lead to wealth, happiness, peace, and joy. Things that were unreachable are now reachable because of my prosperity angel. Faith angels, guardian angels, healing angels, be ye dispatched in the name of Jesus the Christ, who lives within me. Thank you, God-in-me, for the visitation of my angels. My mind, my thoughts, the words that I speak are being transformed and renewed every day.

I now see myself as God sees me: Perfect, whole, complete, divine. I now see the greatness of God, the potential of God, coming forth in me continually, daily, being my supply. God-in-me, manifest yourself in me, through me, as me, in Jesus' Name. Amen.

Prophetic Word

All things have already been worked out for your good. Trust in your guardian angels as they lead you into the secret place of the Most High.

About the Author

Bishop E. Bernard Jordan is your most trusted name in prophecy. In 1989, he predicted the 2005 Gulf Coast natural disaster, storm Katrina, that had a devastating effect on the people in New Orleans. The Master Prophet has prophesied to literally millions of people. He has traveled to Swaziland, South Africa, and delivered the Word of the Lord to the Queen and the Royal Family. He has prophesied in many nations, including Germany, Canada, Korea, and throughout the Caribbean, bringing a clear word of counsel to the leadership of those countries.

He has been featured on NBC's *Today Show,* FOX 5, *Good Day New York,* CNN, and various other networks. He was also featured in *The Daily News, New York Times, New York Post* and *Newsday* with some of his congregates as well as in an interview in *Billboard* magazine on his views concerning social issues. His life-changing messages on reformation and liberation have sparked acclaim, as well as controversy, as he teaches the mystical truths of God's Word. He is the founder of Zoë Ministries in New York City, a prophetic gathering with a vision to impact the globe with Christ's message of liberation. Bishop Jordan has written more than 50 books including best-sellers, *Mentoring, Spiritual Protocol, What Every Woman Should Know About Men, The Power of Money,* and *Cosmic Economics,* and *New York Times* Bestseller, *The Laws of Thinking: 20 Secrets to Using The Divine Power of Your Mind To Manifest Prosperity.* He holds his Doctorate in Religious Studies and a Ph.D. in Religious Studies. He and his wife Pastor Debra have five children. You can watch him live on television on *The Power of Prophecy* telecast or through live streaming, just visit his site at www.bishopjordan.com.